DRAGONFLY
Thinking

Keith –

Thank you for
your fine endorsement
of my book and for
enabling me to share some of
its teachings at NCCU.
Here it is – for your enjoyment and
to share with family members
who might benefit from it.

– Bruce

What people are Saying about
Dragonfly Thinking

An award-winning entrepreneur tells you how to succeed in your career by becoming an accomplished problem solver. He explains techniques he has uncovered to think beyond the bounds of our normal lives. Reading this book will open your eyes to new possibilities in your professional world.

--TROY NAGLE, PHD, MD: PROFESSOR AND FOUNDER OF THE JOINT BIOMEDICAL ENGINEERING DEPARTMENT AT UNC CHAPEL HILL AND NC STATE UNIVERSITY AND FORMERLY PRESIDENT OF THE IEEE, THE LARGEST TECHNICAL SOCIETY IN THE WORLD

Innovation drives the economy, and this book drives innovation.

--JERRY BAKER, PHD: EXECUTIVE DIRECTOR, SIGMA XI THE SCIENTIFIC RESEARCH SOCIETY, RESEARCH TRIANGLE PARK, NC

Dragonfly Thinking breaks through the clutter and gets to the heart of what it takes to solve problems and succeed!

--D. KEITH PIGUES: DEAN, NORTH CAROLINA CENTRAL UNIVERSITY SCHOOL OF BUSINESS AND AUTHOR, WINNING WITH CUSTOMERS: A PLAYBOOK FOR B2B

Struggling with how to solve problems? Bruce Oberhardt's *Dragonfly Thinking* can help!

--MARIA RAPOZA, PHD: VICE PRESIDENT, SCIENCE AND TECHNOLOGY PROGRAM, NORTH CAROLINA BIOTECHNOLOGY CENTER

Lately, new graduates from reputable universities are coming into the workforce missing some of the analytical capabilities that I would expect. This is a worrisome situation and one that Dragonfly Thinking is tackling head on. Read it and live it – it has the potential to change your life.

--Bud Whitmeyer: Chief Executive Officer, dWise Corporation

Students and early careerists will find Dragonfly Thinking valuable for its approach to determining what constitutes a problem and how to frame it, how to analyze problems thoughtfully, and how and when to avoid the limitations of initial unsuccessful attempts at solutions.

--Eliza S. Robertson, Library Director, National Humanities Center

They don't teach you "Dragonfly Thinking" in school, and that's a shame. Innovation that creates wealth or improves the quality of life depends on solving big problems in the real world. This book will open your eyes to a different way of thinking so you can approach problems with a fresh and creative perspective.

--Robert P. Lowman, Ph.D., Associate Vice Chancellor for Research, Research Professor of Psychology, The University of North Carolina at Chapel Hill

Dragonfly Thinking highlights how the first step toward solving any problem is to overcome myopic thinking. By illustrating how to address problems using a multidimensional, multistep approach, it provides the tools you need to unlock your creativity and craft solutions for even the most seemingly intractable problems.

--John Hardin, Executive Director, North Carolina Board of Science & Technology

The best employees are the best problem solvers, and this book shows you the way.

One of the great losses for our children, who have grown up in an educational system that stresses multiple choice test taking, is that they have not been taught how to problem solve or think through a complex situation. *Dragonfly Thinking* provides a road map for training Generation Z graduates now entering the work force on how to tackle these situations and succeed.

While many first-time entrepreneurs focus on their technology as the key to their ultimate success, the truth is that the technology will only be valuable if it helps someone else solve a problem. This book helps build skills for creative problem solving and encourages a practical approach to innovation. It offers useful insights for anyone interested in taking a good idea to the next level.

PROBLEM SOLVING FOR A SUCCESSFUL FUTURE

DRAGONFLY
Thinking

BRUCE OBERHARDT, Ph.D.

Dragonfly Thinking: Problem Solving for a Successful Future

Published and distributed by:
BJO Biomedical LLC
www.bjobiomedical.com

ISBN: 978-0-9848385-2-3 (print, soft cover)
ISBN: 978-0-9848385-3-0 (e-book)
Library of Congress Control Number (LCCN): Pending
Printed in the United States of America

Illustrated by the author

Edited by Matthew A. Oberhardt, PhD

Dedicated to Mindy

ACKNOWLEDGMENTS

I would like to thank Orna Drawas. Her help and advice set the stage for my writing and for moving this book forward. Thank you, Matthew Oberhardt, my editor, for your suggestions on good writing and sources for writers, for your insightful and comprehensive editing, and for improving this book. Thank you, Lynne Kaplan, for your critical eye and organizational suggestions going forward. Thank you, Andrew Oberhardt, for your clever insights on solving difficult problems and your ability to spot typos that escaped the scrutiny of everyone else. Last, but not least, I would like to thank Tom Stevens, the first person who suggested that I write a book. Thank you, Tom, for your mission-oriented perspective and incisive and helpful comments.

Table of Contents

Table of Figures

Smiley Face Puzzle
Dragonfly Terrain Diagram
Smart Car
ROBOCAT
The Next Singularity
Seize the Day!
SUCCESS PATH
Final Dragonfly

Preface

I solve problems, and here is my book.

I wrote this book to address a problem. Many jobs are being threatened or displaced with the continual adoption of new technology. Workers trained in specific skills are rapidly finding their skills outdated, and more than ever before, technology is reshaping the types of challenges that workers face. In the future, these changes will only come faster.

Probably the very last job to be displaced will be that of the employee who is acknowledged as a good problem solver. In fact, many of these individuals will generate economic growth and create new jobs. Some will start new companies. Others will help their current companies adapt to today's unique challenges. Problem solving will become increasingly critical as the pace of adoption of new technologies increases. Problem solving is a skill with a bright future. Unfortunately, people are not being trained in real problem solving as they used to be.

Over the years, I've read many books about outside of the box thinking, and about its application to solving business problems. Although much of what I've seen is informative, a good deal is also theoretical and difficult to apply directly to the challenges of a modern workplace. This is where I saw a real need, and felt I could step in.

During my career, I have tackled and solved many complex biomedical technology and business problems and have participated in many successes. I've positioned myself multiple times at the interface between technology and business, in large companies that I worked for and in founding successful companies and in helping to manage and develop others as well as in consulting for companies and organizations, both large and small. I've seen much of what works and what doesn't. However, I have not seen much written on how to develop superior problem solving skills and specifically to bring them into the complex landscape of a business, especially if there is an entrenched culture. Doing so can be key to creating value and pushing forward at the early stages of your career. This book is intended to fill this void.

As a final thought, I believe that this book should be read first, and then it can serve as a reference. The other way around may not be nearly as useful.

Good luck – and happy problem solving!

To think like the dragonfly...

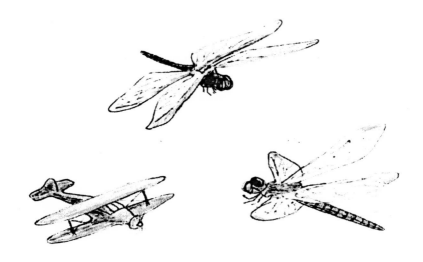

Dragonfly Thinking

Reveals that another view

Is often needed

We must move away

To a different vantage point

Again and again

Since things may not be

As they first appear to be

Let us look anew

Part 1:
Early Experiences with Dragonfly Thinking

1
Problem solving for success

How do you become successful? What is success anyway?

Success can arise from many basic talents, such as a singing voice, entertainment skills, athletic ability, or superior business acumen. But these talents alone do not create success. Success usually requires years of hard work, of crafting nascent talents into true virtuosity. If you have a talent or an unusual ability you must be extremely dedicated in order to develop and perfect it.

One type of skill everyone, regardless of innate talent, can build is the ability to tackle and solve difficult and important problems.

One of the greatest problem solvers of all time is Albert Einstein. Dr. Einstein was voted "The Person of the 20th Century" by Time Magazine from a list of the 100 most important people compiled by a team of world class experts. During his lifetime, Einstein set out to work on a few extremely difficult but important problems. His solutions to these problems changed forever the field of science and the way we view the universe.

My book may not teach you to become another Einstein. It will, however, teach the value of solving problems – especially important ones. It will also teach you how to identify problems that are worth spending a great deal of effort on. Finally, it will help you develop your problem solving skills, and it will show you how to harness the skills of others to tackle important problems, creating value and potentially significantly advancing your career or your business. Solving important problems can be a life changing experience. Solving important problems can also provide a great sense of gratification and happiness.

Helen Keller – an American author, political activist and lecturer, and the first deaf and blind person to earn a Bachelor of Arts degree – said:

"Many persons have a wrong idea of what constitutes true happiness. It is not attained through self-gratification but through fidelity to a worthy purpose."

Solving important problems can be such a purpose.

The key to problem solving is thinking. To solve the most difficult problems, we must therefore be willing to put in the effort and seriously *think*.

Thinking generates new ideas. And ideas transform. Ideas empower. Ideas can astonish and inspire. Often, new ideas are necessary to solve existing problems, since old approaches have been shown to not work. But despite its importance, how often do we deliberately take the time to *think*? Is thinking by itself even enough?

The answer is *no*. Effective thinking requires a good and deliberate strategy; otherwise, you can spend a lot of time thinking in the wrong directions, and get nowhere. If you want to expand and sharpen your thinking while tackling difficult problems, the first step is choosing a strong framework in which to do it. This is what I provide you in this book. In these pages, you will learn an approach I have developed over many years during my own career, through the ins and outs of facing and solving many types of problems, which you can use to focus and guide your own thinking. I call this approach **Dragonfly Thinking.**

And here's how it all started…

My First Biomedical Problem

In my junior year at college I was quite dissatisfied with my studies. As a major in chemical engineering, I was learning how to optimize the output of chemical processing plants to make more profits for my future employers. To me, there was nothing at all creative or inspiring about this curriculum. I was dejected and not sure what to do. I was not a quitter, but I kept thinking that I had entered the wrong field of study.

This all changed when a fraternity brother of mine took me to visit a laboratory in the Electrical Engineering Department. This lab, funded by a gift from a wealthy alumnus, was open to any student or group of students who wished to do their own project in their spare time. Al Conroe, the head of the lab, met with me and asked if I wanted to do a project, and I said I did. I wasn't sure though what it would be. Al said: 'I have the perfect project for you.'

Al met with me in his office and said point blank that last year he had a heart attack and almost died. He elaborated that it was not the heart attack that almost killed him but the blood thinner drug that was used afterward. This drug, warfarin, lessened the ability of the blood to clot but had to be monitored. The drug caused him to bleed internally, and he almost bled out.

The tests that the lab was doing to monitor this drug *stunk*, as he put it. He told me that after he had recovered he visited the lab and watched them perform this test, a test called prothrombin time, and he couldn't believe what he saw:

A technician placed a tube of blood plasma in a water bath to bring it to body temperature, and then added a liquid reagent. He started a stopwatch and then, every few seconds, lifted the tube out of the water bath, tilted it, and placed it back in again. The technician repeated the tube lifting and tilting process until he visually observed a clot forming in the tube, like a blob of gel. He then stopped the stopwatch and recorded the elapsed time. This was the clotting time (aka prothrombin time) that was used to determine the next dose of warfarin.

As Al put it: 'this is a test from the dark ages that has no business being used to monitor patients: the temperature is poorly controlled, the clot difficult to spot, and the whole thing is prone to human error. There should be an electronic instrument performing this test. Here is a project for you.'

I was so excited; I went home that night and dreamt about the project. Here was an important problem that I could make a real contribution on. I had all kinds of ideas even before I went in the next day to work on it. But with all of my grand dreams of automated instruments and clot sensors, I realized once I got into the lab that I had no idea how to actually do any of it. I was totally stumped on my first big problem…

The impact of problems

Life is filled with problems. We experience them in our personal lives as well as in our careers. If you are like most people, the work that you do presents continual problems. When you solve a small problem at work, you are doing your job. It is expected. When you solve a larger problem you are securing your position.

When you solve a really **Big** problem, however, people take notice. It's the solving of the Big Important Problems (**BIPs**) that propels your career and advances it.

A struggle with a big problem, as difficult as it may seem, is usually the necessary step before any major success. And your next success may well be the next important advancement in your career. Advancement is not thrust upon you. *You earn it by solving problems.*

Careers do not advance linearly. They involve rises and falls and plateaus. You can propel your career upward by tackling and solving difficult problems. Solving problems can be energizing, especially when you find solutions. Solving a big problem is work well done. If you solve one or more important problems in the workplace, you will likely be called upon to tackle others.

"The reward for work well done is the opportunity to do more."

-- JONAS SALK, AMERICAN MEDICAL RESEARCHER AND VIROLOGIST, BEST KNOWN FOR HIS DISCOVERY AND DEVELOPMENT OF THE FIRST SAFE AND EFFECTIVE POLIO VACCINE

BIPs are the problems whose solutions can generate great value, either by increasing product output or quality, by treating disease, by extending life, or by accomplishing other worthy goals, depending, of course, on the problem. BIPs are also very difficult to solve; otherwise someone else would have already solved them. Why do you think they're so difficult to solve? Sometimes new knowledge or approaches are needed to solve them. Often, they require a new perspective on old facts. Most ground-breaking scientific advances fall into this category. For instance, this was the case with the development of a polio vaccine.

Solving difficult but important problems

All of the approaches to solving difficult but important problems can be lumped together as tools – tools that the mind can use. With the mind's tools, you can learn how to see problems from different vantage points, angles, and perspectives. If you identify an important problem and determine that solving it will significantly increase value, the actual solution once implemented will most likely also help your own career advancement. The very first step you can take is to learn to identify, and validate the importance of, an important problem.

The next step is actually solving the problem, and in doing so you can harness thinking skills using simple processes that may even come to you quite naturally if you approach the problem in the right way. The name I have given my own approach, which I share in this book, is **Dragonfly Thinking.**

Dragonfly Thinking and this book

By the end of this book, you will be empowered to approach difficult problems, and to solve them.

Part 2 will teach you how to apply your mind towards difficult challenges, focusing on a number of simple problems and brainteasers. The focus here is the *micro* side of dragonfly thinking – the thinking you'll do many times in attacking any complex problem you'll face. As shown in the later Chapters, there are perceptual prisons and white elephants that make it difficult for us to understand problems and that impede problem solving, especially in complex and often important problems in the workplace or in business. Understanding and overcoming these obstacles is often half the battle.

Next, in Part 3, we will face the issue of selecting an important problem to solve in your organization or business, and navigating the often tricky landscape of your business environment to get to a point where you're able to engage the problem. This process involves seeking out and studying a problem, validating that the problem is important, and also finding an experienced person in your organization as a champion or sponsor (as explored in Chapter 11).

Given a complex problem, the *micro* level of Dragonfly Thinking isn't enough. You must also learn how to structure your entire problem solving approach, at the *macro* level, if you are to be successful in solving the problem you've chosen. This process involves brainstorming, interacting with knowledgeable peers, and making and following a master plan until your problem has been solved. This is the focus of Part 4.

Some problems simply are too big, or too complicated, to be managed alone. In these cases, Dragonfly Thinking must be extended to teams. In Part 5, you will learn how to generalize all of the approaches taught earlier into a team atmosphere, how to run effective meetings, and what kind of colleagues to look for. You will learn what kind of role *you* should take in team problem solving, depending on your specific knowledge about the problem you are solving. You will become a master Dragonfly organizer and delegator.

Finally, there is the future. Problem solving will look different as we move further into an increasingly technological age, and I deal with some of the ramifications in Part 6.

So let's go! Let's jump into the role of the dragonfly! It will be a trip into the mind... an exploration of what it takes to *think* deliberately about difficult problems, and to come to completely novel solutions.

But first... How did I solve that first biomedical problem, anyway?

My First Biomedical Problem: Case Study revisited

I set out to work on the prothrombin time project the very next day. Al suggested a possible approach to measure when the clot forms. It didn't work, so I thought of others.

I tried everything I could think of. With each I learned something new about clots, and had more ideas about how I might be able to detect them. Eventually, I discovered that I could illuminate the test tube from the bottom, and when the clot formed the light became much brighter. This seemed like a promising lead.

But now I was stuck again. I saw something that could help but had no idea how to use this to achieve a successful solution. It then occurred to me that I needed to learn more about electronics and how to build an electronic circuit to detect the change that I noticed when a clot forms. Fortunately, there was Al and also other people in the lab from whom I could learn.

Viewing from the side enabled light scatter to be measured, and after some suggestions from others, I built a very simple electronic circuit in a temperature-controlled box which could perform prothrombin time tests. This was a big hit in the lab.

In the two years that followed, I continued working on the prothrombin time testing instrument. Eventually I patented it, along with an approach to automate the system. It was my first patent. I filed it myself without a patent attorney. The work was also published, and the university sent me to give a talk at an international conference. Oh yes, I did graduate with a degree in chemical engineering; but I continued on in graduate school majoring in biomedical engineering with electrical engineering as one of my minors.

During my career in industry that followed, I took on many other problems, some purely biomedical and others at the interface of biomedical technology and business. Years later, however, I returned to my first biomedical problem and rethought it to help advance the field of monitoring blood coagulation at the point of care or near the patient, as opposed to in the lab. This became the basis of the first company I founded, and my technology is now saving lives and is used in nearly every major hospital and anticoagulation clinic in the world as well as in some physician's offices and even in the home.

All of that came later. But in everything that followed, I always recalled my first biomedical problem solving experience. I remember being entirely stuck. Somehow, being completely engrossed in a problem of importance and having Al as a mentor who cared propelled me forward. The process of reasoning that I used for that problem, as well as for many other problems that have I have worked on since then, is what I have termed *Dragonfly Thinking*.

Part 2:
Fundamentals of Dragonfly Thinking

2

Loosening your mind and taking control

My First Dragonfly

I saw my first dragonfly when I was four years old. I was at lakeside with my father, and there were lily pads, frogs, and iridescent flying creatures I had never seen before, darting about in the air above the edge of the lake and sometimes hanging motionless above the water. My dad pointed out a few dragonflies and explained what they were as I looked on in wonder. Suddenly, one of them catapulted up into the air from a reed, stopped in midair, and zoomed away. It was the beginning of a lifelong fascination.

How can you perform beyond what others believe you are capable of? How can your business or company – whether you are self-employed or an employee in a Fortune 500 company – do better through your efforts? The typical answer is to work harder; but is that enough? Is it really possible to sustain a heightened effort over a long haul without it becoming a strain on other parts of your life?

An alternative answer is to become more organized so you can accomplish more work in less time. There are countless books, manuals, and training courses on this approach. Yet another answer, and the subject of this book, is to break out from usual patterns of thought, and discover creative and often even simple and logical solutions to problems. Then you can **perform** what may appear to others as great achievements. You can gain admiration and credit for what you have done. But how can you accomplish this? How do you attain such success?

Look at the world differently

The key to achieving problem solving success is *looking at the world differently*. This is tied to the process of invention. The objective of problem solving is not necessarily to invent things, i.e., things that can be patented (although this is a possible result), but rather to invent and implement new approaches that wouldn't have otherwise been thought of.

In the pages that follow, you will learn concrete methods for stepping outside of your boundaries and seeing things differently during problem solving. You will learn to lead others in examining, clarifying, and achieving goals. There are simple approaches you can use to achieve problem solving success, creating value and career advancement. Knowing when these approaches are called for and applying them to problems in the workplace is the focus of this book.

Some working definitions

Some definitions follow, not dictionary definitions but working definitions. It is important to differentiate between **decision making** and **problem solving**:

Decision Making – choosing the one option that will yield the most favorable outcome, given a number of possible choices.

Troubleshooting – correcting a situation in which an ongoing process has an unexpected failure.

Problem Solving – finding a satisfactory solution to a dilemma, a puzzle, a perplexing situation, or an impediment to growth or to progress, given no apparently good options.

Innovation – creating something new that can be actualized, typically in the physical world. Innovation often but not necessarily results from solving a problem.

Decision making exists in Nature. Swarms of honey bees, for instance, have been studied for their complex group decision making. Analyses of the honey bee swarms show how scouts advertise a dozen or more potential nest sites using a form of dance and how the swarms of bees then reach a decision as to which of the alternative sites is the most desirable for colonization. Unlike complex decision making, however, complex problem solving appears so far to be an expressly human endeavor.

There is also a class of challenges that fall in between problem solving and decision making, called *troubleshooting*. While this type of challenge is often referred to as *problem solving*, I make the distinction here, because the problems that are often encountered in complex business or technology environments are often much more open-ended. Troubleshooting typically comes in when there is a malfunction in a highly controlled process or system, such as when something suddenly goes wrong in a manufacturing plant or with a computer system.

Dragonfly thinking in action: A first taste

Later, in the next chapter, we will go explore some of the reasons why we don't usually think most effectively when attacking problems, and will go over strategies to overcome some of these obstacles. But first, I want to give you a taste of what I mean when I say *Dragonfly Thinking*. Therefore, we will next attack two simple problems: the *kayak problem* and *the nine dot problem*.

These problems are by no means big or important, but they will give you a feel for what's coming later in this chapter and beyond. If you read on, you will learn concrete strategies to expand your own thought processes outside of the ordinary, limiting patterns. But enough for now – on to the problems!

The kayak problem

Andrew is paddling his kayak downstream in an evenly flowing river at 5 miles per hour, relative to the river, and the river is flowing at 2 miles per hour, relative to the shoreline. Andrew accidentally drops his hat into the river but doesn't notice it until 15 minutes later.

As soon as he realizes that he lost his hat, he spins the kayak around in a split second and proceeds upstream at the same paddling speed: 5 miles per hour. How many minutes later does Andrew reach and recover his floating hat?

Can you solve it? Hint: To solve this problem, you can imagine that you are a dragonfly hovering high over the floating hat and watching the entire event. To obtain the most from this exercise, you should actually try to come up with an answer... and without using a pencil.

Solution

This problem may appear to be a complex distance, rate, and time problem. But actually, that is a trick. This is a problem about *perception*, not *math*.

Humans think about distances and speeds primarily in a two-dimensional frame, as our ordinary reference is the plane of the Earth. This two-dimensional space orientation is a type of patterned thinking that limits our perception. One way to approach the kayak problem, however, is to imagine yourself like a dragonfly and approach the world three dimensionally. You can soar to a high vantage point and view the river down below as a thin strip of what looks like a solid, somewhat shiny substance with occasional puffs of white.

If you were hovering in space far above the river, what would you see? You would see Andrew's kayak moving away from his hat. The river would look like a conveyer belt moving Andrew and the hat both relative to the shoreline. You could even swoop down and sit for a while on a floating log in the river and realize that, from a vantage point moving at the speed of the water, it would take exactly as long for Andrew to paddle the kayak away from his hat as to paddle back and retrieve it. The answer would be no different if you were sitting on a log or hovering up above, so the answer is 15 minutes. It will take Andrew exactly the same time to paddle toward the hat as it took in paddling away from it in the first place.

To understand this better, consider Mindy walking at some speed in the aisle between the passenger seats on a moving train. If she drops her hat and realizes 15 seconds later that it's missing, it will take her exactly 15 seconds, walking back towards the hat at the same pace, to reach it. The fact that the train is moving has no bearing on the situation. But the important thing isn't the train or the river. The **Bottom Line** is that, when you break away from thinking patterns based on ordinary experiences, you have a very powerful cognitive advantage. This is the essence of Dragonfly Thinking.

Nature's Ancient Marvels

Why do I like dragonflies? For many reasons! Dragonflies are amazing creatures.

Dragonflies are such phenomenal fliers that they can stay motionless in the air, fly forward, backward, upside down, sideways, and even fly into a spider's web to grab prey and then fly out backward. Dragonflies can fold their legs like a basket and swoop down to catch almost any insect that flies. They can even catch multiple insects on a single dive. Some dragonflies mate in the air, sometimes for hours, often with one dragonfly in the pair resting and the other flying. According to the online Smithsonian Encyclopedia, the dragonfly is the fastest flying insect and can fly up to 35 miles per hour!

Little escapes the scrutiny of a dragonfly, an amazing flier and observer that can reposition itself repeatedly in a short time to take full advantage of its three dimensional environment. And this leads us to our next problem...

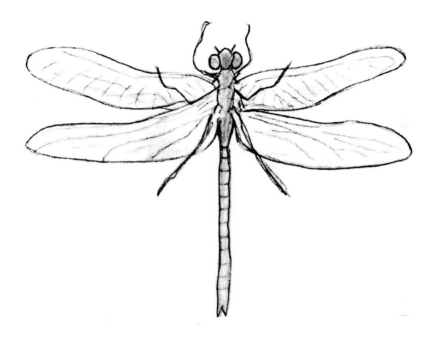

DRAGONFLY OVERHEAD

The nine dot problem

Let's explore another brainteaser. Have you ever seen the nine dot problem? The figure below illustrates it. Your goal is to connect all nine dots with no more than four straight lines, and without lifting the tip of the pencil from the paper:

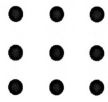

In looking for a solution, we are tempted to draw lines through the three dot arrays. The square formed by the dots is a comfort zone, and we have a tendency to stay within it. We learned this within-the-lines thinking in kindergarten. Staying inside of the square, it is possible to connect all of the dots with five straight lines, but not with four.

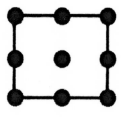

ATTEMPTED SOLUTION

A diagonal line, the fifth line, will connect the center dot to the rest. So, it is fairly easy to connect all of the dots with *five* straight lines without lifting your pencil off of the paper. To connect all of the dots with only *four* straight lines, however, involves going against the usual comfort zone, as is shown in the solution that follows.

Solution

Thinking like a dragonfly, you are not confined to a two-dimensional space. You can move almost anywhere. Lines and perceived squares do not confine you, so you can explore extending lines beyond the nine dots. In the solution, only four straight lines are used. You can start at the **upper left dot** and draw the line from left to right across the top three dots and then continue *beyond the boundaries of the square*. This sets the stage for the next straight line: a diagonal line that connects two more dots diagonally, etc.

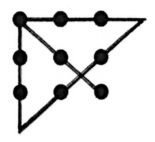

This result is counterintuitive; but if you develop an intuition for seeking counterintuitive approaches then you will have a much greater chance of success.

Now, can you take the nine dot problem to the next level? Can you solve it using only three straight lines without lifting your pencil off or the paper? See if you can find a way to do it. Remember that as a dragonfly you can zoom in for a closer look. When you confine yourself to a plane you are limited, so think like a dragonfly and move in all three dimensions. If you look at the nine dots from way up high or even better (hint) from very close up, can you perceive anything different?

DRAGONFLY EXAMINING THREE DOTS

The secret to this three line solution to the Nine Dot Problem is that the dots are not idealized points: they are actually dark circles. Although they appear small from a distance, they do have measurable diameters. By taking advantage of this fact, you can draw a slanted line that runs through all three dots in each column. This enables three straight lines to connect all of the dots without lifting your pencil off of the paper. If the dots had smaller diameters, your lines would need to be longer, but you could still solve the problem—even if your lines would have to extend off the paper.

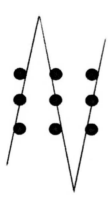

SOLUTION TO THE NINE DOT PROBLEM USING THREE STRAIGHT LINES

Now, for the final question, can you connect all of the nine dots using only one straight line? Can you find the answer using Dragonfly Thinking?

Looking for a Solution to the Nine Dot Problem using One Straight Line

As a dragonfly, you are not confined to a two dimensional planar world. You can see things from different vantage points. You can fly down to observe the paper upon which the dots are drawn. You can hang motionless in the air and observe the paper closely. You can see that the paper has an edge, and it is thin like a leaf on a tree. If it is thin, it can bend or curl. It can be folded into a scroll. So what if you curled the paper by rolling it up into a scroll or a cylindrical shape? What then? How does this help? As you can see from the figure that follows, you can still have a single straight line on the paper, but by rolling it up this line can intersect all nine dots!

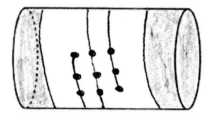

PAPER WRAPPED AROUND CYLINDER AT THE APPROPRIATE ANGLE OF INCLINE ENABLES
SOLUTION.

Is this cheating? Are these straight lines? Yes, the lines are straight, on the paper (in two dimensions) although the paper is curved in three dimensions. If you were to unfurl the paper again, the lines would be perfectly straight in all three dimensions. The lines will end, of course, where the paper ends in the direction of travel of the lines. Curving the paper, such as using a cylindrical shape, allows the ends of the paper to be coupled together so that a line drawn in one direction will circle the cylinder and return near its point of origin. Believe it or not, there are also other solutions using one straight line!

Breaking out of our patterns

The solutions to the Kayak Problem and Nine Dot Problem illustrate how our thinking is often restricted or confined. The solution to a problem is sometimes out of reach, because our minds do not let us go there. When we finally see the solution, we may say "Eureka". When we finally see our old habitual patterns for what they are, we can often break through to the outside and get some fresh air.

3

Why aren't we usually in the dragonfly zone?

Alright, now we've seen some dragonfly thinking in action. So why is it that we don't always think this way, if it's so much more effective for solving difficult problems? The reasons are many, and we will go into them now.

Thinking, in General

We would like to believe that we think first and then act. However, during the course of a normal day, most of us operate by a routine or routines consisting of reflexive behavior. How often do we actually take the time to slow down and **think**? When you take a shower, do you really *think* about it? Probably not. Most of us just take the shower. We do it! We act! We follow a routine, because if we thought about each step in the process, we would never make it to work. Thinking is slow, and gets in the way of rapid action, which is necessary for mundane tasks. In some sense, deliberate thinking and efficient action are almost diametrically opposite one another. Therefore, in a situation in which good performance is judged by efficiency – such as getting to work on time – thinking is a detriment.

When thinking gets in the way, we suspend thinking. This can be an extremely useful trait. However, we can suspend thinking so often that it is easy to become lazy and avoid it, even when it's most useful. Rather than think, we can become trapped in invisible patterns of behavior and thought, and we can have trouble escaping these routines when novel thinking is called for. In problem solving, we must go beyond reflexive behavior, and **think deliberately.**

Dragonfly Thinking is all about breaking free of our reflexive behaviors, of our habitual thought prisons, and freeing our minds to explore options that we would usually overlook out of habit. So let's take a look at the walls of these prisons our thoughts are stuck in, and chart them. Let's see if we can map out their features and perhaps even their weaknesses. Once we know what we're up against... well, then we have a real chance at breaking free.

Perceptual prisons

Little do we realize that we are not only confined by cultural norms in the environments around us, such as in the workplace (which we'll go into a bit later), but we are also entrapped by limitations in our ability to perceive things that we see or hear right before our very eyes and ears. Sometimes what we think we remember is not really what happened. Also, there are certain things that we don't perceive unless our brains are appropriately primed.

Reticular Activation

There are times when we are persistent, when we are diligent, and when we hear the right advice, and yet we are not yet ready to receive it.

The reticular system in the brain is responsible for our attention to certain cues. Say you just bought a Volvo automobile, and you're driving along. Suddenly, you might notice a ton of Volvos on the road. You'll think to yourself, "Hey, I never realized that there were so many Volvos out there!" This is because of the reticular activator effect of purchasing a Volvo. The brain is now primed to see Volvos, whereas before they were invisible to you. We are constrained by our brain and senses as well as by cultural norms in the workplace. A solution to a problem can be right in front of us, but if our brain is not conditioned properly, we may never notice it.

Most of us like to think we are always aware, yet our brains often deceive us. Developing an enhanced awareness of how the work environment and the mind can distort a problem is a valuable and critical skill.

Thumbs Up

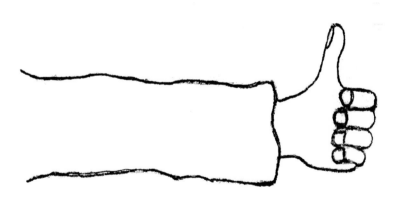

Try this experiment. Make fists and give the thumbs up sign with both hands. Hold your thumbs together at arm's length, allowing your two thumbs to touch. If you now stare at your two thumbs held together, you will see all of the fine details of both thumbs.

Your thumbnails will be clearly delineated, along with the cuticles and other features of each thumb. Now, stare intently at your right thumb and move your left thumb about six inches to the left. You will continue to see all of the detail in the right thumb, but not in the left thumb. In fact, as you stare intently at your right thumb, you may barely notice that there is still a left thumb. The thumb exists as a bulk image, but that's it. If you bring your left thumb back to its former position next to your right thumb you will again see all of the detail in both thumbs. What we are focusing on makes all the difference.

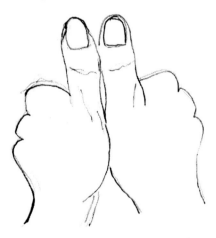

What we really see is not what we think we see

This happens because the retina in the eye has a tiny spot in the center of the visual field, called the macula, where nerve endings are most densely gathered. This one little spot is what perceives detail. Outside of this tiny area in the visual field there is very little detail. Yet, we walk around all of the time thinking that our entire visual field is filled with detail. Our brains deceive us. Visually, we perceive an illusory world, yet we do not realize it.

Attention works much like visual perception. We can be focused on one solution, or one type of solution, or one way of thinking, so hard that we can't see any others. In business, we often have certain expectations, and sometimes we believe that these expectations are being met when in fact they aren't.

McGurk Effect

The McGurk Effect is an extraordinary example of fooled perception.

The McGurk effect is a multisensory phenomenon first described in a paper by Harry McGurk and John MacDonald in 1976. The effect comes about when a video is played, in which a face repeats a single noise several times. In the *audio* track, the noise is *Ba*. In the *visual* track, the noise is *Ga*. If both the *audio* and the *visual* are turned on, the noise that the viewer hears is neither *Ba* nor *Ga*, but *Da*! The mind automatically combines the two confused signals – audio and visual – *Ba* and *Ga* – into a new sound, which is what the viewer literally hears. The effect is most striking if you close your eyes between each repetition of the sound, in which case you will hear something like "*Ba, Da, Ba, Da, Ba, Da.*" The effect is amazing!

This is a simple, yet powerful demonstration of the ability of our perception to be fundamentally deceived by what is around us.

Many optical illusions also highlight the ability of our senses to be tricked. What we see is, in some cases, *quite literally* determined by what we expect to see. To step outside of this we must extricate ourselves from ordinary thinking and be ready to view problems from entirely unusual viewpoints.

Can You Read This?

Aoccdrnig to rscheearch at Cmabrigde Uinervtisy, it deosn't mttaer in what oredr the ltteers in a wrod are, the olny iprmoatnt tihng is taht the frist and lsat ltteer be at the rghit pclae. The rset can be a total mses and you can sitll raed it wouthit a porbelm.

Tihs is bcuseae the huamn mnid deos not raed ervey lteter by istlef, but the wrod as a wlohe.

Amzanig

The above lines of text show yet another example of visual perception: how we read words and sentences. This example shows how the eye and brain can enable us to decode garbled text, yet this built-in ability can cause us to miss juxtaposed letters and typographical errors.

Fooled by Memory

I remember being at a meeting that went something like this:

Nancy: "Is that a good price?"

Jeff: "Yes, it's the lowest out there. I think we should go with it. "

Nancy: "I'm still not convinced – it seems high. Did you check a few vendors?"

Jeff: (typing away on his laptop): "I did, and I tabulated a list. Here, I'll send it along to you and Sharon."

Two weeks later

Nancy: "Sharon, I'm working up the sales projections. Did Jeff ever email you the pricing information? I could have sworn that he sent it to me, but I can't find it..."

Sharon: "I am sure I received it. Just a sec..." (checking her computer) "... hmm... maybe I didn't. That's weird..."

Were you ever fooled into thinking that something took place in a way that it actually didn't?

So what's the take-home lesson from all of the examples in this chapter?

That we are constrained and sometimes fooled by our brains, by our senses, and also by invisible patterns defined by our daily routines and our work. Transcending these requires a deliberate effort to think differently.

4

Fenced in by invisible walls

Many problems are very tough to solve because we are being held back by unseen forces. We are constrained, fenced in, and we don't realize it!

Often, these constraints are the result of cultural norms. The culture of a company is the way things are done and the way people operate. Culture consists of a group of accepted protocols and values that were developed in the past and have, for various reasons, been carried forward. If you work for a large company or organization, those cultural norms can be a big part of what initially made your company successful.

Many of the norms in large companies are in place for good reasons, and have been there for extended periods of time. We often think of them as absolute principles, like laws of physics. However, cultural norms are not everlasting. In fact, the key success principles of companies, like most products, services, and businesses, have finite life spans. What is strange is that we are usually unaware of how many of the constraints placed upon us by the business-as-usual norms are outdated or confining to creativity. Inevitably, the constraints that hinder us, which we cannot see or are perhaps unaware of, are themselves often part of the problems we are attempting to solve. These constraints can confound our attempts to progress to the light at the end of the tunnel.

When a particular cultural norm becomes a barrier, it may be on its way out. Or, more likely, a new norm will be needed to handle the exception that the old norm was incapable of effectively dealing with.

Flash Case Study: The invisible white elephant

Can a white elephant also be invisible?

I was working for a company that had four major divisions: Financial, Marketing, Manufacturing, and Technical. These divisions were housed in separate quarters and did not interact very much. I was in the Technical Division, where we invented new things and made new medical diagnostic product prototypes as well as finished products.

If the Marketing Division liked a prototype product, they would give a green light for it to go forward in the Technical Division, where it could be further developed. After that, the product could be sent on to Manufacturing, and eventually could be produced and sold. This system was reasonable, except in the case of a few really excellent projects we were working on that Marketing unceremoniously canned.

Where was the white elephant? It was the barrier that kept us from speaking with the marketing people early on. Why was it invisible? The invisibility was a norm or constraint that we couldn't see. I complained to my boss about this after Marketing killed a particularly strong project I was working on. He replied that this was the way the company did things, because senior management didn't want to influence creativity too early in the process. *Hogwash*, I thought. My boss, however, had a friend or two in marketing and arranged for a marketing person to drop by early in another project I was working on. This amounted to a breakthrough, and in effect, a new policy for the company.

It turned out that not just me, but also my colleagues in the Technical Division were eager to learn what would be needed for Marketing. Now our considerations included a more complete picture of the customer – a new vantage point – and I believe that this positively influenced our creativity. In addition, the marketing person came away with an understanding of what was possible from a technical standpoint and what wasn't. This led to ongoing mutual feedback on a periodic basis. Everyone in our division liked this approach. It was a resounding example of the power of identifying white elephants, and relocating them to the jungle of obsolete animals, where they belong.

Nobody Sees the White Elephant

Businesses *often* have large, white elephants in the room where everyone works. Everyone walks around them, never bumping into them, giving them plenty of space. Despite their size, their smell, and their occasional noises, they can remain entirely invisible. These elephants form a workplace's cultural norms.

White Elephant in the Workplace

A new employee must learn to walk like the others, avoiding the white elephant. But what if a memo were issued saying that the white elephant will now be removed? People could now walk through the space where the elephant used to reside, saving the annoyance and wasted time of going around it. This is in effect why some companies ask employees for suggestions to improve productivity. But this is often not enough, especially if the employees making the suggestions can't see the white elephant in the first place.

While this scenario might seem farfetched, the proverbial white elephant is often a huge presence in companies: ever-present and yet barely-noticed. This barrier can eat up a lot of people's time and effort. Finding and removing white elephants is often the reason that outside consulting firms are hired. The work of seeing and removing white elephants is highly valued, but extremely difficult for those ensconced in the company's culture.

A culture of complexity

When you start to work in an organization, over time, you begin to see how things are done. At first, a simple task may appear as a brainteaser if you are not familiar with the organization's procedures. These procedures can form a sort of *hidden logic* that must be followed to operate effectively in the organization. These hidden logics are patterns that can help you be effective, but can also hinder you. It is important to learn them, but to also be aware that they are there, and to think of whether they could be changed or improved.

An 11-year old girl named Olivia gave me the following complex brainteaser.

Question: How do you put an elephant in a refrigerator?

You might answer: First you find a very large refrigerator.

Olivia's Answer: First you open the door; then you put the elephant in; then you close the door.

Question: How do you put a giraffe in a refrigerator?

You might answer: First you open the door; then you put the giraffe in; then you close the door.

Olivia's Answer: First you open the door; then you take the elephant out; then you put the giraffe in; then you close the door.

Question: There was a big animal convention. Animals came from all over the world to attend. One animal, however, did not attend. Which animal didn't attend?

You might answer: Let's see – probably the sloth, because he's slooooooow.

Olivia's Answer: The giraffe, since he was locked in the refrigerator.

Question: How do you cross the stream in the jungle and not get bitten by the crocodiles?

You might answer: It is simple; you search for a part of the stream with no crocodiles, and then you run across.

Olivia's Answer: You just walk across. You do not have to worry about the crocodiles, because they are away and attending the animal convention.

In Olivia's brainteaser, it is not obvious at first that the different parts of the brainteaser are connected. When you begin to suspect that they are connected, it may still be difficult to learn the type of logic that connects them. This may be similar to the logic used in an organization. Once you understand your organization's logic, you will find it much easier to tackle complex problems that arise within it. You also might become aware of ways that the hidden logic is hindering progress, or creating its own set of problems.

The Giant Hairball

Question: What is all of this talk about patterns, barriers, hidden logics, and white elephants that confine us? *Answer:* It is *reality*. All around us are all sorts of spider webs that confine us but are practically invisible. Many of these webs are built into the workplace.

Gordon MacKenzie says it well in his creatively illustrated book: "Orbiting the Giant Hairball – A Corporate Fool's Guide to Surviving with Grace" – Copyright 1996, published by the Penguin Group, New York, NY. MacKenzie says:

"Every new policy is another hair for the hairball. Hairs are never taken away, only added. Even frequent reorganizations have failed to remove hairs (people, sometimes; hairs, never). Quite the contrary, each reorganization seems to add a whole new layer of hairs. The hairball grows enormous."

He follows by saying: "The trouble with this is that Corporate Normalcy derives from and is dedicated to past realities and past successes. There is no room for original or primary creativity."

Finding and removing white elephants

We should not merely seek to identify and define the barriers around us. We should also develop ways to circumvent them. When you learn how to develop your problem solving skills, various white elephants become visible and can then be removed. Often this will lead to an improvement in the business or greater efficiency or possibly even solving a **Big** problem that nobody else has solved that may create considerable value.

"Insanity: doing the same thing over and over again and expecting different results."

— ALBERT EINSTEIN, CHOSEN BY TIME MAGAZINE
AS THE MOST IMPORTANT PERSON OF THE 20ᵀᴴ CENTURY
(SEE COVER OF TIME MAGAZINE, DECEMBER 31, 1999)

The quote by Albert Einstein is repeated often to illustrate that a new approach must be tried if the old one is not working. This quote has a flip side: if we wish to solve Big problems, we need to get out of our old mindset in order to do it!

I know an executive, named Joseph, who put this Einstein quote on his desk so it was in his view all of the time. He saw it so often that he began incorporating the philosophy into his daily routine. When confronted with a company practice, he would ask his boss, Sandra, why it was done that way. She would usually reply: "Well, I guess it's just what we've always done!"

Joseph began examining many company procedures and trying to understand their rationale. Sometimes he found a very good reason for why a particular procedure was to be carried out exactly as specified. When there were extra steps that were unnecessary, Joseph sought ways to reduce or to simplify them. Other times, however, he found that an entire procedure was unnecessary or outdated.

One of the procedures that Joseph came across was a manual filing procedure that clearly had been developed before computerized files and back-up data storage. Joseph developed a new filing system that was quickly adopted, and ended up saving the company time and money. For Joseph, this became a passion. He enjoyed doing it and was rewarded for each success, which motivated him to continue the process with even greater passion. For his efforts, Joseph was eventually promoted to Director of Engineering of his company.

Where we must go

We are constrained, and as a result our vision and our ideas are limited. When we have the right understanding of how to solve problems, we can achieve miraculous results. We must develop our ability to identify new goals and to synthesize appropriate approaches for realizing these goals. The rest is execution, and this is what most companies and many individuals do best.

5

Complex problems

Previous examples of Dragonfly Thinking were applied to simple brainteasers. Brainteasers are good exercises to cultivate the ability to solve problems, but perhaps more than anything, they demonstrate the importance of stepping beyond ordinary logic. In the real workplace, issues or problems that must be dealt with are often complex. They may be intricate and have many parts, some of which can be addressed by simple logic and some of which cannot.

Obvious and Unobvious Solutions to Problems

In the business world, ordinary logic may be sufficient to solve a problem once the correct information is assembled. Sometimes, however, logic alone will not yield an effective solution. In such cases, there is usually an unobvious step that must be recognized or uncovered.

Case study: attempting to achieve market dominance

This is an actual case study of a situation that took place more than 40 years ago. The names of the companies involved are omitted and are not relevant, since both companies merged with other companies well over a decade ago. Those currently in the medical diagnostics business may not even know about this interesting case that resulted from a battle for market dominance. We shall call these companies *RivalInc* and *TrenchCom*.

RivalInc was the market leader in the automated **blood chemistry** analysis field. A well-known industry powerhouse, RivalInc was rapidly growing, and had a superb technology for performing analysis on the liquid portion of blood (serum or plasma) but not on blood cells.

TrenchCom was the dominant player in the automated **blood cell** analysis field.

RivalInc had its eyes on TrenchCom's market.

I should note that these companies were leaders in a new industry, automated clinical laboratory diagnostic testing. This industry had very high growth at that time, because the products made a lot of money for the customers: hospitals and clinical labs. When you manufacture and sell a product that in addition to satisfying a need or requirement for the customer also makes money for this customer, you have a big winner. In this industry, at that time, there was great customer demand for these products.

In studying the automated blood cell analysis systems manufactured and sold by TrenchCom, RivalInc learned that TrenchCom's products had a lot of moving parts and frequently needed part replacements or repair. RivalInc had an automated analysis technology with very few moving parts. RivalInc recognized that if its technology could be applied to blood cell analysis, the resulting products would have very few moving parts and consequently would have a much lower frequency of repair than TrenchCom's products. This would translate to a market advantage for RivalInc. RivalInc wanted to become dominant in TrenchCom's market and had a plan to do just that. RivalInc wanted to eat TrenchCom's lunch.

RivalInc developed its first cell analysis product. This effort took a number of years, involved a lot of top notch technical employees and consultants, and was one of RivalInc's largest projects ever undertaken. The product was rigorously tested against TrenchCom's product in house, and it was determined that RivalInc's new cell analyzer was far more reliable than the product from TrenchCom, the current market leader. RivalInc initiated a limited product launch at a number of major leading and prestigious hospital clinical laboratories. These clinical laboratories already had TrenchCom's product in routine service and were willing to test RivalInc's product alongside it.

At the end of the trial period, RivalInc surveyed each clinical laboratory about how things were going. They expected to hear that their product was much more reliable than TrenchCom's. However, they learned much to their dismay that none of the hospital clinical laboratories were using their product any longer! RivalInc's product was now sitting idly, gathering dust. The clinical laboratories told RivalInc that their product broke down too often, so they had taken it out of service. With this following the results of their in-house tests, in which RivalInc's product clearly outperformed TrenchCom's, RivalInc was astounded. What had happened?

The actual behind the scenes story in this case study demonstrates creative problem solving on the part of TrenchCom.

TrenchCom was not sleeping. As an entrenched competitor, they knew the limitations of their technology and of their product. They also knew that RivalInc was coming after them. In addition, they suspected that RivalInc would try to outperform their product with its own. When RivalInc launched its product at a number of high profile, well-known hospital clinical laboratories, TrenchCom got busy.

Field service personnel from TrenchCom drove vans through the streets of the cities where the comparison testing was taking place. These vans were on the streets at all hours, day and night, and were filled with spare parts and replacement products. When a customer had a problem, they called TrenchCom. A van would then pull up, a part would be replaced, and the system would be up and running in a very short time. Sometimes, the entire instrumented system would be replaced with a new one. Often the clinical laboratory supervisor did not even know that the product was serviced.

Confident RivalInc, on the other hand, would take a day or two or often several days to respond to a problem, or sometimes even longer. Their instrument's problems were far less frequent than those of TrenchCom's instrument, but to the clinical laboratory supervisor, TrenchCom's system was seen to be almost always in service, while RivalInc's product would be down for extended periods of time. The net effect was that RivalInc's system was viewed as less reliable than TrenchCom's product, when actually the opposite was true.

To this day, it is reported in the industry archives that RivalInc's products were less reliable than TrenchCom's and that is why RivalInc lost the battle for the blood cell analysis market after challenging TrenchCom.

Was TrenchCom using Dragonfly Thinking? RivalInc surely wasn't.

One could imagine that TrenchCom may have had numerous

meetings, perhaps involving some of their most creative people, when they realized that RivalInc was coming after them. They were well aware of the shortcomings of their products and also of the technology that RivalInc used and what they would be up against. They may have recognized that their biggest weakness – that of frequent breakdowns – would be in the spotlight when RivalInc introduced its products. One could imagine further that they knew there was no time to improve their products and that a battle for market domination had already begun.

Perhaps they looked at the situation from the vantage point of an observer in the laboratory when an automated instrument stopped working. They might have thought like a Dragonfly, hovering about, watching the lab workers bustle about. "When a system is down, what do we do now?" they might have asked. One solution to this problem, and in fact the one they implemented, was to restore the automated instrument to full service so quickly that nobody (except the fly on the wall) would notice that it had ever malfunctioned or had broken down in the first place. This creative problem solving won the battle and the war.

Large vs. Small Organizations

It is important to recognize that large organizations are different from small ones. A large organization is like a large ship. It tends to be slow moving and makes wide turns. A small organization can move quickly and turn on a dime.

In the vast majority of large organizations, employee risk taking is discouraged, since it can cause instability. There is a great deal of groundwork to be done to convince others of the importance of an idea and approach. *Buy-in* is needed at each stage of problem-solving (identification, definition, and implementation of a specific solution), from your coworkers as well as those above you and below you in the organizational structure. Learning to obtain buy-in is a key skill in getting traction for your ideas.

Despite all these difficulties, there is often more time in a large organization both to define a problem – since it is not going away any time soon – and to work on it. Large organizations typically have far more resources than small ones and are more stable. Larger organizations can weather the storm at sea better than the small one, so you have the luxury of time to pursue big problems that might otherwise be too ambitious.

In a small organization, and especially in a venture backed company, there isn't time to obtain buy-in. Everyone is working hard to paddle the boat or it will sink. New ideas and new solutions are readily sought and will usually be implemented immediately. It is both easier, and more urgent, to develop solutions *fast*. Although the implementation is easier, the time pressure can often hinder creativity.

Middle market or mid-size companies are intermediate in size between large and small companies. These companies tend to be growth oriented and account for about 40% of employment in the US. Depending upon the stage of growth and size, middle market companies may tend to operate more like large or small companies. Learning the character of your company is key if you are to identify, define, and solve BIPs.

Flash Case Study: New Instrument Development

A few years back, there was a venture-backed company with strong engineering and life science talent that needed a new instrument as part of a product offering. The team consisted of industrial veterans experienced at designing and building new things. A decision had been made to develop a microprocessor-controlled instrument in-house and to hire a suitable software expert to complete the development team for the instrument. Procedures were in place to move forward quickly. I was asked by an investor to review this decision.

After examining the effort needed to develop the new instrument, I came to realize that there were better options. From a referral source, I obtained the name of a vendor that had appropriate software expertise on staff, and that could both develop and manufacture the instrument. An analysis showed that this vendor could develop the instrument in 60% of the time and at 80% of the cost, while freeing up personnel in the venture-backed company to do other things. The venture company contracted the vendor, and as a result they developed the instrument ahead of schedule. They later negotiated a manufacturing agreement with this vendor, ensuring longevity to the solution. The lesson? When aligned with the culture of a company, solutions can be quickly implemented, saving both time and money.

6

Take home lessons

Advance Goals

How can you do greater things – as individuals – and become recognized for them by your company? A good way is by advancing company goals. Or if you are self-employed, this can mean advancing your own personal or professional goals. These goals cannot be advanced very far if you are constrained and operating inside a cage. Most importantly, many of the ways you can achieve these goals usually lie outside of the specific work that is handed to you.

Define Problems

Defining a problem and understanding it as deeply as possible and from multiple vantage points will best position you to come up with a solution. This is the essence of Dragonfly Thinking. If you define a problem and understand its essence, you will be well on your way to solving it. Often, after a comprehensive analysis a key and previously hidden perspective will emerge. Then the solution may just pop out in front of you.

Sometimes, just a little expertise or information that you are missing will enable you to turn that corner. The internet is a starting point, but any Big Important Problem will usually require the insight of appropriate experts. Be ready to send an e-mail or to pick up the phone and meet someone for coffee who may have the appropriate expertise or information. Most often, attempting to solve a difficult problem will involve meeting a number of people at different times. Many of these individuals are referred by others that you have met.

Be Persistent

When you commit to a goal, it will not be achieved if you slack off on it. How often are the days too long and too busy? How often is it too much trouble to contact or meet with someone? How often do we get sidetracked or bogged down in something else, letting the problem go unsolved? Human beings are subject to distractions. We procrastinate. It is therefore critical to be persistent.

This is especially true in today's world of computers, smart phones, social media, and search engines. Dependence on instant answers can erode our willingness to slow down and *think*. This takes a toll on our progress in solving problems and on our career advancement. When you receive an instant answer or suggestion, it is crucial you sit down and *think* about it. You must verify your information. New knowledge could come to light that contradicts the original data. Be persistent. Remember that, for your Big Important Problem, quality is more important than speed.

"Nothing in this world can take the place of persistence. Talent will not; nothing is more common than unsuccessful people with talent. Genius will not; unrewarded genius is almost a proverb. Education will not; the world is full of educated derelicts. Persistence and determination alone are omnipotent. The slogan 'press on' has solved and always will solve the problems of the human race."

— CALVIN COOLIDGE, 30TH PRESIDENT OF THE UNITED STATES

Part 3:

Finding and Approaching Big, Important Problems

7

Dragonfly thinking in the workplace

Dragonfly Perspectives

Dragonflies have a very wide visual field and sharp eyes that wrap around their heads, so they can see you even after they've flown past you. All dragonflies have excellent vision. They can survey a large area and then easily swoop down for a closer look. The ability to view the big picture from above, hanging motionless in midair, and then to dart down at will to look closely at an object of interest, is what led me to think of the dragonfly as a model for thinking as applied to solving difficult problems.

With a history dating back to prehistoric times, when the oxygen content on the planet was much greater than it is today, fossil records show dragonfly ancestors with two and a half foot wingspans. Over the millennia, dragonflies have adapted, but their fundamental role in nature has not changed. They have always been fliers, and have likely always been able to stop on a dime, grab prey in midair, and see the world from a vast number of vantages. This is to say, dragonflies long ago discovered a great way to operate, and they've stuck with it. And clearly, their method works!

Now that we've laid the basis for dragonfly thinking, I'm going to share my method for applying these lessons in the workplace: a **four stage process** for using Dragonfly Thinking, along with **tactical processes** and **exercises** to help you along. If you learn these **four stages**, you may then apply them repeatedly to help your organization, and your career.

Fundamental Stages for Problem Solving in the Workplace:

1. *Find a BIP*
2. *Study and validate the BIP*
3. *Seek BIP help from an SMC (Sponsor, Mentor, Champion)*
4. *Solve the BIP*

The process sounds simple, but it involves patience and time and tools. We will go through each of these stages in great detail in the coming chapters. Stage 4 is addressed in *Part 4: How to solve Big, Important Problems.*

Mastering the four stages involves:

1. Find a BIP: Develop your skill at identifying Big, Important Problems to work on.

2. Study the BIP: Develop your skill at understanding the details essential for solving Big Important Problems by initiating the process of understanding and also validating the importance of the problem.

3. Seek help from an SMC: Develop the ability to make an appropriate contact with someone higher up in the organization or a thought leader in your business sector. Seek further validation that the problem you have selected to work on is actually a BIP and that solving this BIP will help your organization. Also see if you can obtain assistance in solving the BIP and support in implementing a solution, once the BIP has been solved.

4. Solve the BIP: Develop your skill at solving Big Important Problems. Also, develop your skill at forming a problem solving team when necessary. Learn how to manage the team effort to solve the Biggest, most Important Problems even if they are difficult or complex.

After Stage 4, you can often participate in implementing the solution to the BIP. This participation can take many forms. You may enjoy seeing your work put into action, and you might bask in the improved situation that you helped to bring about. In most cases, you will receive praise for a job well done, and you will enjoy positive reinforcement from others before, during, and after the solution is put into effect.

Did you notice that the first three out of four stages of Dragonfly Thinking have nothing to do with actual problem solving? This is no accident, and it leads to our first general principle:

GENERAL PRINCIPLE A: Think deeply about a problem before starting to develop its solution.

Albert Einstein once said:

"If I had an hour to solve a problem I'd spend 55 minutes thinking about the problem and 5 minutes thinking about solutions."

As usual, Einstein nailed the point right on the head. Finding and then deeply understanding a BIP is the most important groundwork you can do towards solving a Big Important Problem. Too often, we are tempted to jump into problem-solving mode before we actually understand a problem sufficiently. This can be a great waste of time. But this principle is about more than just that: Einstein also understood that the best solution to a problem often will not come from trying to find solutions, but will rather come naturally as a result of gaining a deep understanding of the problem itself. It is inside the *problem*, not in naïve ideas for *solutions*, where the best answers lie.

Even during brainstorming (described in Parts 4 and 5), during which thinking of many possible solutions is critical, deeply understanding your problem will greatly increase the relevance of your ideas. This is why I've presented dragonfly thinking in the workplace as a 4-stage process, in which seventy five percent of the focus is on finding and validating the right problem, and then only the last stage involves 'problem solving' in the strict sense. You should focus your own problem solving efforts similarly.

Keep this general principle in mind as you move forward. Below is an outline of the whole dragonfly process. We will go into great detail on each of these stages in Parts 3 and 4 of this book:

Overview of Dragonfly Thinking:
Find, Study, Seek, and Solve

Stage 1: Find a BIP
Identify the right problem to work on.
Begin to validate that it is a BIP.
> **TACTICAL PROCESS 1:** Develop a master list of problems to be solved
> **EXERCISE 1:** Work on your list

Stage 2: Study the BIP
Validate that the problem is a BIP.
Develop a passion for solving this problem
Consider the problem as terrain.
Fly high above the terrain to survey the problem from all angles.
Swoop low on occasion and hover in a selected location to examine promising areas that could lead to a solution.

TACTICAL PROCESS 2: Validate that solving the Big problem that you selected will be of great help to your organization
EXERCISE 2: Map your terrain

Stage 3: Seek help from an SMC
Generate ideas and see what others (especially an SMC) think about them.
Follow the ideas where they lead you.

TACTICAL PROCESS 3: How to cultivate the ability to develop a relationship with a sponsor, mentor, or champion (SMC)
EXERCISE 3: Make a list of potential SMCs

Stage 4: Solve the BIP
TACTICAL PROCESS 4: An eight-step process for problem solving:
1. *Survey the problem from different vantage points, like the dragonfly*
2. *Use domain experience & generate new ideas*
3. *Redefine the problem & generate more ideas accordingly*
4. *Recombine, link, or add to ideas*
5. *Take a break.*
6. *Consolidate ideas into groups based on similarity*
7. *Rank groups and repeat process*
8. *Select the most likely group, and work towards solution*

EXERCISE 4: Try solo problem solving with a brainteaser

Are you ready?

The first **stage** lays the foundation toward your future success. **Tactical Process 1** deals with something very basic: **making a list of the problems or issues that are already out there as well as new ones that emerge.** So are you ready? Let's begin!

8

Stage 1 — Find a BIP

Identify the right problem to work on.
Begin to validate that the problem is a BIP.

In order to find a BIP, you must know what you are looking for. You must also be certain that it is a BIP. You do not want to expend effort on LUPs (Little, Unimportant Problems). Solving problems that nobody cares about may be considered a big waste of time.

How to find BIPs

1. Typically, people have not come to grips with BIPs that affect the business, and often view them as vague but impenetrable barriers. Sometimes they see about as much hope in overcoming these barriers as in defying gravity. Many BIPs remain unsolved, because they are not seen as solvable.

2. Often, merely asking the right questions will lead to the statement or framework of a BIP.

3. BIPs may be related to: company growth; profitability; finding or retaining customers; quality of products or services; competition; developing new products or services; or other realms. Be open in where you look for these problems.

4. When a BIP is outlined, it can often be restated more precisely, leading to a reformulation of the problem. Restating or reformulating the statement of a BIP may often bring you much closer to a solution. Often, the reformulation of the problem itself is the most important conceptual leap in the process.

5. If you observe and inquire, you will be able to identify existing workplace problems, including BIPs. You might begin by asking questions like: "What are the biggest problems we face as a company?" or "What are our most profitable products?"

TACTICAL PROCESS 1:
Develop a master list of problems to be solved

Many of us have lists of items or actions that must be carried out, i.e., *to do* lists. Some of us carry these lists on our computers or smart phones, while others use old fashioned pencil and paper. In these lists an item or task is crossed off once it has been accomplished. When we carry around a list, we become more efficient, and we are less likely to forget to do something important.

Tactical Process No. 1 in effect establishes a new type of list that we can carry around. This list consists of problems in the workplace or business or organization associated with our work. Preparing such a list and using it enables us to develop an awareness of problems to be solved. Often these problems may be in the form of *issues* to be dealt with. The process starts with an awareness of the problems, especially the BIPs. What should be on this list? The simple answer is, every problem that you think is important and which, if solved, would be of great benefit to your organization.

This list is simply a log of problems that you become aware of and that need to be solved. This is where it all starts. When you begin logging problems, you will begin to look at the world differently. This is an essential first step in finding appropriate BIPs.

It might be overwhelming to imagine solving every problem you come across, big and small. This level of effort, however, is not necessary. You can contribute to your organization and advance your career by solving one or possibly a few choice problems. Sometimes problems are connected in unseen ways, and the solution to one minimizes the extent of another or reveals a more urgent problem that needs to be attended to.

If you proceed as follows, you will develop a new discipline that will open doors and help focus your efforts.

1. List the problems that you see in front of you, and keep adding to the list. Maintain this list. You can carry a special notebook with you to record them or simply use your smartphone, etc. to have them always at hand. As problems are solved or simply go away, either because a deadline has passed or they are no longer important, cross them off the list.

2. Give each problem a rating. An "A rating" means that this problem, if solved, will significantly and positively impact your organization by adding considerable value. A "B rating" means that this is an important problem, and you will be noticed if you solve it. A "C rating" means this is a problem that you have been assigned to work on and is part of the standard workload or must be dealt with during the normal course of work. *Do not hesitate to upgrade or downgrade the rating of any problem at any time.*

3. Pick an "A problem" to work on during your discretionary time. You may not have discretionary time or spare time at work, but it is always possible to meet people for lunch

or perhaps for coffee, and you can think about problems when not at work or when commuting to and from work. Since much of the time solving hard problems comes in simply thinking through all of their angles, commutes can be put to extremely good use. The best problem is one that is extremely important and not time sensitive. If a problem is time sensitive, it may still be worth working on, but you might have more trouble finding a truly novel solution. ***Whereas necessity is the mother of invention, stress is often the enemy of creativity.***

Once you have the list, you can identify the A, B, and C problems. Sometimes, there are so many C problems that you may not want to keep them on this list. In that case, use this special list for A and B problems only. The purpose of the list is to aid in your selection of a problem to work on, hopefully a BIP. ***The best problem is one that you may not know how to solve, but one for which you believe, and ultimately can verify, that it sure would be nice if you did.***

GENERAL PRINCIPLE B:
Choose your problem wisely and remember: necessity is the mother of invention, but stress is often the enemy of creativity.

Choose your problems wisely. Do not pick something with time pressure that will create stress, if you can help it. In business activities or technology development work there are usually time pressures. For a BIP, however, especially one that is not being tackled at the moment with 100% effort, it is always best if there is little – if any – time pressure. If there is time pressure involved, then this is a problem that is not a discretionary time problem but more likely a full time problem.

Naturally, if you are lucky enough to be assigned an important problem to work on by your boss, you can spend a lot of time working on it. In my first industrial job, I worked for a company as a biomedical engineer. My company made analytical equipment used in laboratories. After only two weeks with the company, I was assigned to an important project with two other employees. This project was all about solving an important technical problem, and there was a good deal of time pressure. I have documented the story in Case Study II that follows later on.

Once you have your list, you can identify the A, B, and C problems, and remove C problems if you determine the list feels too cluttered. It is important, however, to be aware of the continuum of all problems in the workplace from C problems to A problems that you should or could deal with and to understand the special significance of solving an A problem. After you prepare this list, it is time to select a problem and to work on it. ***To reiterate, the best problem is one that you may not know how to solve but one for which you know quite well that it sure would be nice if you did.*** All you have to do is to pick one – a good one – a "Big" problem – a BIP – and work on it.

Exercise I: Work on your list

Take 15 minutes for an exercise...

Now that you have reached this point, take a break and put this book aside for a few minutes. You have now read about Stage 1, but to progress further you will need to act.

Start a notebook or computer file to list problems that you identify, especially important problems. It may take only two minutes to do this, but by taking action, you will have started the process and progressed from merely reading to actualizing. Strange as it may seem, the conversion of thought to action activates your subconscious mind and mobilizes you for success.

Later on, after you have thought of problems to place on your list you can assign A, B, or C labels to these problems and then determine which A problem to work on as a long-term project. If you cannot identify the A problems by yourself, as is usually the case, another approach is to ask around. If you speak with people in your organization, you will probably be able to network your way to people who can identify the A problems, i.e. the BIPs.

One suggestion is to give yourself a week to compile your complete List of Problems, network with people, and identify the one to work on. Do you need a week? One person I know completed this task in minutes, since he already knew the most pressing problems facing his organization. Sometimes a key problem is mentioned by someone at a meeting or at a talk given by a speaker from your organization. The essential consideration is to have enough time to create a List of Problems and to keep it at hand and work with it.

Look for the BIPs. Sometimes, what you think is a BIP isn't, and what you least expect is a BIP is. How strange is that?

When you have assembled a list of possible BIPs and have selected one that you think you would like to solve, you have reached the next stage.

9

Stage 2 — Study the BIP

Consider the problem as terrain.

Fly high above the terrain to survey the problem from all angles.

Swoop low on occasion and hover in a selected location to examine promising areas that could lead to a solution.

Dragonfly observation

I was working on my second draft of this book one day in late August, and I decided to take a break just before lunchtime. I went outside for a breath of summer air. The sun in North Carolina felt good. Lots of critters were out. I hadn't seen a real dragonfly in quite a while, and I was just wondering if there were any around that time of year when a large dragonfly materialized.

I was delighted. I froze, watching the dragonfly circle. He flitted about a few times and then stopped, appearing like nothing other than a blemish on the thick air. He then darted to a new location several meters away. He circled, darted again, and hung motionless once more. This time he stayed in one spot for so long that he seemed stuck, and then he suddenly darted away again, stopping short at yet another midair vantage point. I started to wonder what it was he was looking for. Then, all of a sudden, the dragonfly swooped, caught a bug in midair, and took off.

It struck me, just as the dragonfly left, that I had not been the only observer on the porch. The dragonfly, too, had been using his hovering vantages to survey his surroundings, just as I had watched him. I wondered how much more of the landscape he noticed from his shifting vantages. Probably a lot, including me! Certainly, he saw enough that he was able to catch lunch. Which reminded me....

The fundamental approach to finding solutions to BIPs

If there is a fundamental approach to finding solutions to difficult problems, it is to **ask the right questions**. This can be done by asking questions that pop up when you view a situation differently. Many times, this comes down simply to asking questions that others are embarrassed to ask, because they assume that everyone already knows the answer. Never assume such a thing. As with the earlier brainteasers, imagine looking at the situation from different perspectives: high up, close up, on the fly. You can consider the task of finding a worthy problem as one of finding a pesky mosquito. For example, you can ask: "what is most bothersome in the organization but is difficult to do anything about?"

Asking the right questions is a learned skill. If developed and sharpened, it can open new doors and lead to buried treasure and professional growth. It is often quite easy to solve a problem if the right questions have been asked. Insightful questions reveal the essence of a problem or issue and make it easier to solve.

Simply asking the right questions may in some cases almost completely reveal a valid solution to a difficult problem. For example, you can ask: "Why do we always seem to have this particular problem? Or "What is the reason that nobody has eliminated this barrier to success?" Or: "Why hasn't this been a priority for the company to solve?" Or "Do you have a way to deal with this issue?" Or "What is the most important problem that you typically have to deal with?" Each of these phrasings will reveal a different perspective on the same problem. On the other hand, it is possible to be deceived by others if they choose to provide evasive answers. This may happen especially if interests are not aligned.

Alignment of interests

Mother: "Jeremy, do you have a test this week?"

Jeremy: "No Mom".

Mother: "Are you sure? You've been playing a lot of video games, and I better see you studying if you do have one."

2 Days Later

Mother: "Jeremy, I thought you didn't have a test this week. How come Jenna did? She's in your class, right?"

Jeremy: "Mom, it wasn't a test. It was a quiz."

In the case of an actual problem or issue of importance, it is hoped that nobody is trying to be deceptive or evasive. In business, however, people sometimes are evasive, and in some cases they may not be helpful at all if they think that helping you in your efforts or answering your questions is not in their interest.

The best way to achieve alignment of interests is to make sure that all who are involved understand how they will benefit from the problem solving effort, especially if the problem you are working on is solved. Consider that you will have to deal with WIIFM (What's in it for me?).

TACTICAL PROCESS 2:
Validate that solving the Big problem you selected will be of great help to your organization

It is important to determine that you are working on a BIP—i.e., that your problem is sufficiently important—and in fact that the BIP is considered a BIP in your company, business, industry, etc. One way to validate the importance of your problem is to ask other people, especially those who should be in a position to know.

Typically, when your choice of BIP is validated by someone who is higher up in the organization, it is a good indicator that you have selected an important problem. Validation may also come from a peer. It may simply be someone who has the appropriate information because their job intersects with one of the central issues in the problem, or because they know someone else who has useful information.

When the importance of the problem has been validated you will feel a certain level of comfort, since you are now on the right track. Even so, continue to validate. This will increase your comfort level. If, on the other hand, a person who is in the know does not consider the problem to be important, this calls for additional investigation before expending further effort in trying to come up with a solution.

Ongoing Example: Trouble with Feedback

Let's consider the example of Marty who works in the Publications Department for a household appliance manufacturer and is trying to use Dragonfly Thinking. We find Marty at the stage of validating the importance of a problem that he has become aware of and also trying to understand it better. He is currently meeting with Cecilia, who was referred by a colleague in the Sales Department.

Marty: "Bill suggested I speak with you about customer feedback – specifically about what's been tried and why it didn't work."

Cecilia: "We do get some very good feedback, but it isn't easy." Sometimes it can feel like drilling for oil. If a product isn't working we hear about it immediately, but if there is something that could be improved or a feature that would be nice to have, we rarely, if ever, hear back."

Marty: "What have you tried?"

Cecilia: "We've contacted customers by phone, mail, and e-mail; we've sent short product evaluation forms; and we've even conducted focus groups. Customer feedback is still a problem."

Marty: "Do you know why we're having so much trouble getting information back from them?"

Cecilia: "Not really. Our customers are busy. If the product works they move on."

Marty now thinks he is no better off than he was before he started asking questions. He knows what was tried and what has failed. Cecilia appears to have written off other approaches, since the customer appears to be so busy that the only feedback the company is likely to hear is about a product that is broken.

Marty doesn't realize that Cecilia's impressions represent an outline of the problem, only, and a barely visible outline. The substance of the problem has not yet been revealed. Should Marty abandon this problem and work on another instead? That would be easy to do. But selecting another problem which was not the first choice to begin with may not be a superior approach. Time and effort has already been invested in the customer feedback problem. A different problem would require similar effort. In the end, it could end up in the same place. What should Marty do?

Your Success Depends Upon *Culture*, Not *Structure*

As you are aware, organizations have organizational charts, spelling out the chain of command. This includes essentially all companies as well as all other organizations: governmental; nonprofit; and for profit. The organizational chart, however, is not a pathway that will automatically furnish you with BIPs. It also won't necessarily facilitate finding the solutions to important problems, nor the implementation of solutions to problems you have solved.

It is important to recognize that a company actually functions via its **culture**, not its structure. The structure is a model, only, one that conforms more or less to other organizational models. The culture is how things really get done, how people interact, how the norms of interchange operate, how news travels, how cooperation is nourished and sustained, and how business problems in healthy companies are actually identified and solved.

If you identify an important problem to work on you will rarely, if ever, do so through the company's formal organizational structure. If you ask for permission to identify an important problem or to work on a problem of importance in your spare time, and this problem is not part of your boss's agenda or priority list – as is usually the case – you may create the impression that you have too much spare time and be assigned more work. This can actually be detrimental to your solving a BIP in the organization. Moreover, you will not have time to develop and hone your problem solving skills for the future. Therefore, it is important to use your *discretionary time*, including lunches and coffee breaks, as well as time away from work (when appropriate), in order to contemplate and progress on your BIP.

In the end, if you do your assigned work but also solve important problems for the company, your boss will also benefit and will be grateful. Long before the success of a solved problem is made public, you will want to inform your boss, emphasizing that the work you did was in your discretionary time as well as on your own, non-company time. The best time to speak to your boss about the problem you took on as your own and your success in solving it is right after you report on and hand in all of your assigned work. You can then say: "Oh yes, there is this other thing I've been working on, too..."

Trouble with Feedback: Studying the BIP

Marty and John, the Marketing Manager, are meeting in John's office:

Marty: "As Marketing Manager, I bet you know all of the customer-related problems that the company faces."

John: "I wish I knew all of them."

Marty: "I heard that customer feedback is a problem. Is that true?"

John: "We do get feedback, and sometimes it's good feedback. I would say that in the majority of cases, the responses from customers aren't really a problem."

Marty: "Hmm, I was at this marketing meeting and came away with the idea that we weren't getting enough feedback from customers."

John: "Yea, but it is really a matter of timing. In many cases we don't hear back from customers soon enough, even though we actively seek their comments."

Marty: "So perhaps the key, then, is developing a way to get feedback sooner and from more customers. Do you think that'd be helpful?"

John: "I do. If we could achieve that much, it would be very helpful! Cecilia can tell you what approaches have been tried, but if you want greater insight into why things aren't working, you may want to speak with Brianna from Sales. Here, I'll connect you two via email."

Marty has validated the problem he is about to begin working on. John thinks it would be great if this problem were solved. Marty has also learned that Cecilia is a resource person but that she does not have the insight into the customers he is seeking. His discussion with Cecilia has already borne this out. Marty now believes he should talk to Briana. The stage has been set. The rest is up to Marty.

Beware of over-simplicity

In my first industrial job, I was once told by one of my boss's peers that: **"For every complex problem there is always a simple solution, and it is wrong!"** I always remembered that. In my experience in years that followed, I have found this statement to be almost always true.

Rarely is there a simple solution. Even if there is, finding it may not be simple. Usually, it is necessary to compile a lot of information before you can solve a problem. You can employ Dragonfly Thinking to come up with different views of the problem and to ask atypical questions. You will obtain new information about the problem and often something unanticipated will emerge. When you do this it will inevitably lead to a different view of the problem and to a solution.

Flash Case Study: No New Customers in Sight

A nanotechnology company had positive cash flow but was unable to find new customers to expand its business. Most of its revenue came from one big customer. The company decided that, in order to expand its customer base, it should develop new, high margin products in the medical field. They pulled me in as a consultant to help develop novel medical devices and to expand the business using the company's current technology. The company was absolutely convinced it had found the solution to its growth problems. This had become an entrenched dogma.

Before jumping into device development, I stepped back and analyzed the situation the company was in, speaking to many people at different levels and going over various records. My analysis showed that, although the company's technology could be used to advantage in medical devices, their simple solution was not so simple. They were not structured properly to develop and refine medical devices. It would also take a long time to develop medical devices, and there was another, easier and simpler and less risky way. This was to add value to existing products and technologies from other companies through technology-sharing collaborations, rather than to develop their own new products from scratch. New customers could come in the form of companies who could benefit from using the technology in their own products, rather than by my client trying to enter a new field entirely.

I visited several senior managers from other companies, with whom I had contacts, to assess the value that my client could add. Subsequently, I initiated conference calls with interested parties, enabling my clients' best minds to interact with the prospective customer. This led to confidentiality agreements, material transfer agreements, and detailed discussions of problems that my client might be able to solve in products under development. The interactions led my client to the new customers they sought.

In addition to the new customers, I learned through this process of a relevant trade show that my client had been unaware of, which I attended along with a senior technical manager. Several new customers were in attendance, and were able to act as on-sight referral sources to help us recruit additional new customers. In all, my solution, born from Dragonfly Thinking, was successful.

Trouble with Feedback: The Sales picture

Marty is meeting with Briana from Sales, after being introduced via email by John:

Marty: "As Sales Supervisor, I bet you know a lot about customer-related problems that the company faces, and especially why it's so difficult to get customer feedback."

Briana: "Have you been speaking with John?"

Marty: "I have, and also Cecilia. John was the one who suggested I speak with you."

Briana: "I knew John was involved. He's the only one I discuss this issue with. I'll be glad to help – what would you like to know?"

Marty: "Well, I was wondering if you have any intuition why we are having trouble getting useful information back from our customer base?"

Briana: "More customer feedback would be very good. For one thing, it would help our sales effort. For another, it could help us, along with other information that we have, to improve our products. Although I've contacted customers and spoken with them and even conducted a few focus groups, we haven't really gotten much useful info. I concluded that we were just spinning wheels, and that we've gotten just about all that we're going to get."

Marty: "Have you exhausted every method that's available? How about internet surveys, or special promotions. Or perhaps starting a twitter feed for specials and deals, and asking for feedback?"

Briana: "We haven't tried those approaches, but I don't think that they'll give us anything useful. I've been told that years ago our customers knew a lot more about our products than they do now. Now, they sell so many items that they know next to nothing about each one."

Marty: "Can we educate them?"

Briana: "No, it won't work. They don't have time."

Marty: "Is there no way to solve this problem?"

Briana: "There's no way that I know of. If you think of one, please let me in on it."

Marty: "You said that we used to get feedback from them. Isn't that right?"

Briana: "Yes, but that was a long time ago – before I was working here."

Marty: "Is there anybody else I can talk to about this, especially about how it used to be, perhaps someone who has been around here for a long time?"

Briana: "Well… Jack, our Chief Operating Officer has been around for quite a while. I've heard he's approachable."

Marty has now obtained new insight on the problem he's working on. Briana has helped to redefine the problem for him. This problem, however, now seems impossible to solve. It's up to Marty to be persistent and to continue to gather information in order to find a solution.

Should Marty set up a meeting with Jack? Jack is pretty high up in the organization. Marty has heard through the grapevine that Jack has the CEO's ear and that he was responsible for firing the cafeteria staff last September. What if Jack thinks that Marty is wasting time on a problem that can't be solved, and that he should be doing other things with his time? Now that he believes he is dealing with an important problem but one that may be beyond everyone's reach, what should he do?

EXERCISE 2: Map your terrain

Try taking 15 minutes to do this exercise:

First, take a problem you are working on — hopefully a BIP — and map it. That's right; take a piece of paper, say letter or notebook size, and draw some terrain. You can begin by drawing an idea web relating different parts of the problem, and their subproblems, to each other. By the end, you'll want to divide the terrain into several sections, representing different aspects of the problem.

Just the act of mapping out the terrain will likely give you new ideas. However, take the next step and try viewing the map from afar, upside down, etc. You can place the map on the table or stand over it on the floor. You should have the whole terrain fresh in your mind after mapping it, so this exercise may help you generate new ideas. Write down any idea that comes to mind, whether you think it is relevant or not. If there is a window behind the drawing when you look, perhaps the window will stimulate some thoughts. You can ask: "How will this window help me solve the problem?" "What if it were open?" "How could an open window help?" etc. Remember, each of your thoughts is also symbolic and connected to other thoughts. Perhaps you are practicing this exercise outside, and a tree may be staring at you. You can ask yourself: how can this tree help? This is a seemingly illogical leap, but where will it take you? Perhaps the shape of the leaves will remind you of a potential collaborator's logo, and you'll jot down that idea. Let your creativity reign. Allow the presence of the tree into your thought process, as you contemplate the problem landscape.

After several minutes or when the ideas cease to flow, look at the terrain diagram and at the list of generated ideas again. See if any new ideas come to mind, and write them down. When you are finished, a lot will probably have changed. Your mind is now reprogrammed, and the diagram and ideas can be revisited later, for example the next day, to see what new insights will emerge. Your subconscious mind will still be working on the problem, long after you think that you have stopped. But remember: you must actually perform the exercise. Merely reading about it will not be very helpful.

10

Stage 3 — Seek help from an SMC

Generate ideas and see what others (especially an SMC) think about them.

Follow the ideas where they lead you.

Big Dragonflies

I recall seeing dragonflies that had wing spans of about 6 inches in the Outer Banks of North Carolina, the most eastern, coastal part of the state. I couldn't believe how large these dragonflies were.

I was in a sea kayak in the Pamlico Sound between the Outer Banks and the mainland, traveling along trails of water between the tall reeds and other high foliage. I had wandered quite far from shore. With brushes and low plants clogging my view more than a few feet in any direction, I turned a bend to a sudden clearing, with a tall, rotting tree in the water set on top with an Osprey's nest. It seemed a very magical and remote setting. I was drifting in place, enjoying my private watery glade. Then, I suddenly saw dragonflies.

There were big dragonflies and small ones, and some monstrous ones, the biggest I had ever seen. The whole troupe of them hovered about, snatching up prey, alighting on the water, or standing still in the air, like a bunch of magicians. The whole scene was just fascinating. For me, it was a rare glimpse into the dragonfly world and perhaps the dragonfly hierarchy.

For the rest of the day, I saw many dragonflies. They were there in the reeds, along the low edges of the water, by sandy embankments and mounds of estuary mud. But the ones who struck me most were the gigantic ones. They appeared near the other dragonflies like some sorts of leaders, perhaps dragonfly kings or princes, and other dragonflies seemed to be following them. Sometimes when a huge one took off, a few little ones followed.

Maybe in their dragonfly brains, the little guys had exactly the right idea. In that moment, to me it seemed perfectly obvious. Follow the big ones. After all, having gotten so big themselves, the gigantic dragonflies surely must have known where they were going. It befitted the little ones to take cues from them, in the hope that one day they would be that big themselves. I pondered this as I continued back to shore. Just as there are big dragonflies, there are big people, important people, powerful people. Some of these people could advise you or guide you on your quest to identify and solve a BIP.

Working definitions — SMCs

Some definitions follow, not dictionary definitions but working definitions:

Sponsor – An individual who agrees to provide resources to help you.

Mentor – An individual who helps you with your career.

Champion – An individual who wants to see it happen or help make it happen.

Obtaining help from powerful people

At some point in the process of attacking a BIP – often, after you've validated that the problem is important – it is appropriate to communicate with a Sponsor, Mentor, or Champion figure: an **SMC**. The **SMC** is typically a person who is more experienced and has more responsibility and authority than you in your organization, or sometimes outside of it. Sometimes you will seek out an SMC, and other times you will develop a relationship with one through normal actions in the company or extra-work activities. SMCs are crucial for getting traction with your ideas.

It is important to approach a potential SMC in the correct way. The impression you want to make is that you would like to learn from him or her or get in contact with other people who might help your cause, rather than that you want to get help from him specifically.

Tactically speaking, instead of asking if the SMC can provide you with help, you should ask if he *knows a person* who could answer the question that you are asking or could provide help. Treat it as a networking meeting, rather than a supplication for aid. This will avoid putting the potential SMC in an awkward position of being asked to become a sponsor. If the SMC wishes to sponsor your quest, he will do so. Otherwise, he might direct you to another potential SMC.

It is best to meet a potential SMC at a time when he (or she) is winding down, such as the end of the day or perhaps after 4 PM on a Friday. It is often best to meet him in his office. You may also wish to take notes.

I often ask if I can take notes when I sit down for a meeting. Almost nobody objects to you taking notes. Furthermore, a person is often flattered to learn that what they say is important enough to be written down or entered via keystrokes. It is likewise important to make frequent eye contact. If you succeed in obtaining an SMC's blessing, you will now have obtained a sponsor who will materially help, a mentor from whom you can learn, or a champion for your cause.

Should you worry about being scooped by your SMC? If a senior executive steals your idea, typically everyone will know, since you would have had prior discussions with others. Although it is generally unlikely that people will be dishonest in this manner, and it would therefore be a rare event, in some organizational cultures this could happen with little or no consequence for the dishonest person. It is important to understand the culture of your organization for avoiding such unfortunate cases. However, even in the worst case scenario, you will have learned from the problem-solving process, and you will certainly have other ideas in the future that can be shared through other avenues.

TACTICAL PROCESS 3:
How to cultivate the ability to develop a relationship with a sponsor, mentor, or champion (SMC)

When you have selected a problem to work on, it is important to validate that choice. Is this really a problem worth your time and energy? Will solving this problem help your organization? How can you be sure at the end of the day, when you have solved it, that anybody – especially those who count – will care? An insurance policy is needed. This is one of the great benefits of finding an SMC. Here are some pointers:

1. Make sure that there is a sponsor, mentor, or champion, e.g. an official at a higher level in your company or organization who recognizes the importance of the

problem you are working on. Note, this individual does not have to know right away that you have selected this problem as a major undertaking.

2. When you have made significant progress in your efforts and believe you have a solution at hand, share this information with your potential SMC.

3. The next step may be that you are asked to present your solution to someone else or to give a presentation to a small group. Be ready and willing to do so.

4. Take all feedback or suggestions that might be made into consideration. Any solution or approach that you may come up with is subject to improvement.

5. The rest will evolve in time, and often it will provide recognition and lead to new opportunities.

What is the best way to present yourself to a potential SMC so that you will increase the probability of gaining support? To achieve the desired results, should you employ selling tactics or should you simply try to act natural? This issue is critical, as it could spell the difference between successfully solving a BIP versus having the idea frowned upon or canned. Therefore, I've devoted the next chapter specifically to this.

11

Impressing big fish: how to hook an SMC

PLEASE NOTE: Although the focus of this book is not on communication, some of the things I have learned over the years follow. The focal point of this advice is on capturing the attention and interest of a potential Sponsor, Mentor, or Champion (SMC), but this advice applies equally well to communication in general, and to many other parts of life.

Classic Advice

Dale Carnegie, in his classic book" "How to Win Friends and Influence People" (first Copyright 1936) offers the following advice on ways to make people like you:

1. Become genuinely interested in other people.
2. Smile.
3. Remember that a person's name is to that person the sweetest and most important sound in any language.
4. Be a good listener. Encourage others to talk about themselves.
5. Talk in terms of the other person's interests.
6. Make the other person feel important – and do it sincerely.

Dale Carnegie also has advice on techniques for handling people:

1. Don't criticize, condemn or complain.
2. Give honest and sincere appreciation.
3. Arouse in the other person an eager want.

Ray Daley's Authenticity

I met Ray Daley in 1992. I was the Founder and Chief Scientific Officer of a venture backed medical device company, and my investors hired Ray as a consultant to work with the C-level executives (such as CEO, CFO, etc.). Ray was well known in local business circles, since he was a master negotiator and had recently started a leadership development company called Wellspring. After almost losing his life to a malignant brain tumor that was then in remission, Ray had left his prior business activities to start this new company and train leaders, something he had always wanted to do.

When I met Ray, I sensed that he was different from other people I had met in business. He exuded no ego, no self-importance. It felt like his main focus was on the other person, and I took an immediate liking to him. Ray had deep insight into people, an ability that had helped him in his business negotiations through the years. Ray was also a great teacher. He said that when you interact with others, the most important thing to create is what he called *authentic presence*.

This is important also when speaking with people in positions of greater responsibility in your organization. The way you present yourself may determine whether you will be taken seriously and whether you will receive the information you are looking for. ***According to Ray, authentic presence is when what you think, say, and do are the same.*** Ray said, "It enhances your ability to communicate successfully with others by being consistent, truthful, proactive, and loving."

Ray Daley's five methods of developing an authentic presence or even better, an "authentic existence", are:

1. **Call upon your courage in dealing with change.**
2. **Place your focus upon the here and now.**
3. **Be progressively refining your communication skills.**
4. **Seek to understand before seeking to be understood.**
5. **Respond rather than react.**

Deal with Change Courageously

Things around us are changing all of the time. It is often unsettling when something you have relied on or assumed is now changed or no longer there. It requires courage to continue with your efforts, with your mission, in spite of this.

In a conversation you may suddenly discover, perhaps as a result of something the other person said, that something that you took for granted has changed. As difficult as this may seem, do not show bewilderment or concern. *Don't* try to hide your natural emotions, but *do* try to go with the flow. If there is something to be concerned about, you can discuss it later on. In a conversation with a potential sponsor, mentor, advisor or anyone, it is most authentic to recognize that your personal issues or so called "hang-ups" do not matter. The only thing that matters is the person you are making eye contact with, and the information they are relaying to you.

Be Here Now

"Be Here Now" is the title of a song by the late George Harrison, a member of the famous British rock group, the Beatles, in his 1973 album, "Living in the Material World". Harrison's song includes the following in its lyrics: "a mind that likes to wander 'round the corner is an unwise mind." Several other songwriters have written songs with the same title since then.

The earlier inspiration for all of this may have come from the cult-hit book entitled: "Be Here Now" that was printed in 1971 and written by Baba Ram Dass (formerly Richard Alpert), a spiritual teacher and author. In addition to the phrase "Be Here Now", serving as the title of his book, Ram Dass uses it as a mantra or slogan to focus on the here and now. He teaches that when the mind begins to wander, you can bring it back by asking yourself: 'Where am I?' and answering: 'Here!' and then asking: 'What time is it' and answering: 'Now!' Being grounded in the present is important if you are to be authentic in your interactions with others.

Become a Better Communicator

Communication is an essential tool, and it can be cultivated. Some people are natural communicators and are able to share their point of view, thoughts, and concerns seamlessly, feeling intuitively when to insert just the right bit of emotion, or when not to. Others find it less natural, and need to nurture the skill. But a little practice here can go a long way.

One thing that can help is to write down the important question or key discussion points before you actually meet the person you'll be speaking with. You can also enlist the help of a trusted friend who is a good communicator to help you phrase your questions or express your thoughts. You can rehearse your lines. You do not have to remember them exactly, but having prepared beforehand, you will communicate far more effectively than if you just wing it. Often, the conversation won't go at all as you planned, but the planning you did will still calm you and keep you focused on the points you wanted to get to. A little preparation goes a long way.

Seek to Understand

It is also very important to recognize that one of the greatest gifts that you can give to another person is – believe it or not – just listening to them. That's right: listening. Really listening, showing them that you are giving your undivided attention – something many of us rarely do – is a great gift to the other person. Too often, we don't listen. Have you ever waited for someone to finish so you can say what you have in your head, and as a result, miss everything they tell you? Not listening has become a chronic problem in our society. We are bombarded by so much audio and visual *stuff* that many of us are conditioned to tune it all out, and to continue to speak without hearing.

Hearing what someone else says, however, is only the beginning, for the key issue is what they are trying to actually convey to you. They may not be expressing themselves well at all; so listen and dig deep to uncover the meaning. Understand. Watch their body language. Don't hesitate to ask questions to obtain clarification of intent. This aspect is also aligned with that of making the other person that you are interacting with your main focus and giving them your undivided attention.

Respond Rather than React

Ray liked to quote Viktor Frankl, the clinical psychologist, therapist, and philosopher, who miraculously survived several Nazi concentration and death camps during World War II. In addition to other accomplishments, Frankl wrote the best-selling landmark book "Man's Search for Meaning," where he describes his experiences in concentration camps, and how he developed his psychotherapeutic method of existentialist therapy (termed Logotherapy). A key principle that kept him sane in the most horrid conditions was that no matter what could be done to him, it was always in his power to choose his response. Frankl refused to react but instead to choose his response, since he always had that power and that choice.

"We who lived in concentration camps can remember the men who walked through the huts comforting others, giving away their last piece of bread. They may have been few in number, but they offer sufficient proof that everything can be taken from a man but one thing: the last of the human freedoms -- to choose one's attitude in any given set of circumstances, to choose one's own way."

— Viktor E. Frankl

Work with your List of Problems

It will become important to communicate with others about the problem you wish to work on or are already working on. I suggested earlier that you should develop a priority list of problems or issues important to your organization. This list will contain key, sometimes fundamental problems, and should be distinct from the typical laundry lists that you might use in your everyday work. A list of two or three top problems is a superb list, especially if you follow through and decide on a single problem to attack first.

It is very important to make a connection with, and speak to, someone higher up in your company or organization. If you are self-employed, speak with a business guru, advisor, consultant, or board member you respect. What you are seeking is a highly experienced viewpoint on both the company and the problem you've selected. Cultivate authenticity in your interactions. Express a sense of purpose. Let your mentor guide you in determining what the most important problems really are.

If you develop your list of "A" problems, you can then try to determine which two or three of the problems on the list are the most important. In this way, you can determine the biggest prizes to shoot for. You may wish to select a good "B" problem first to gain a success and get your feet wet. It's your call. Whatever you choose, make sure that the problem you go forward with is important. It should be one that, if solved, would seem to those high up in the organization as in some way helping with a key company priority.

You may wish to briefly investigate several problems before committing to one. Once you commit, however, it is very important to stick with it until you have made some progress that you can share with others.

You may recall that Marty has obtained new insight from Briana on the problem he has been working on. Briana has essentially redefined the problem for him, but as a result of this process, it now seems impossible to solve. When Marty asked who has been around for a long time and might be able to provide further insight, Brianna suggested that he speak with Jack, the Company's Chief Operating Officer. Marty went back to speak with John, instead.

Trouble with Feedback: SMC recon

Marty and John are meeting again in John's office:

Marty: "Hi John. I spoke with Briana, as you suggested."

John: "Great! Was it useful?"

Marty: "I think it was, but I'm feeling a bit stuck now. Briana said that we've learned about all we can from our customers from the methods we have tried."

John: "Did she say anything else?"

Marty: "Yeah, she said I should speak with Jack, the COO. What do you suggest?"

John: "Hmm... what was her rationale?"

Marty: "Well, she said that things used to be different and they were getting better feedback in the past, so I asked if she knew of anyone who was around then. That's how his name came up."

John: "Jack has certainly been around for a long time, but be careful here. He's a good guy, very strong, but you'll want to be sure you come across well. He's known to make flash judgements, so you want to come prepared and be very well organized when you meet him. I'm sure you'll do fine."

Marty: "Thanks, John, I'll do that."

Marty decides to bite the bullet and speak with Jack. First he sets up an appointment, trying to schedule it for late afternoon and getting his wish. He prepares for the appointment. He writes notes on how he would like to come across at the meeting and what he will need to say. He develops and rehearses an *elevator speech*: a short summary that says all you wish to communicate, but is concise enough to be recited to someone you meet in an elevator between floors. He prepares thoroughly and even brings his notes with him to the meeting.

EXERCISE 3: Make a list of potential SMCs

Try this exercise.

First, think of the people you know or have heard about high up in your organization or your industry or business who could potentially be SMCs. That is, who could *sponsor* your effort on a BIP by providing you with resources, could *mentor* you by helping you with your career, or could *champion* your problem solving effort because he wants to see a solution. If you don't have a BIP that you're working on, that's okay; you can still think of an SMC who might be helpful for a range of BIPs. Make a short list. This should not take long, perhaps five minutes.

Then, the next time you meet for lunch or coffee with someone familiar with the problem you're working on, ask who he or she thinks would be a likely SMC. Again, you can ask this question even if you don't have a specific BIP—it's still a helpful exercise to get a gauge for who you might potentially approach if needed. See if your list can be validated by others and if there are perhaps other SMCs that you overlooked. Sometimes the best SMC is someone you would never have thought of.

This exercise starts on paper but moves into the real world. By exerting the effort to make a list, you are focusing your attention and thinking and also activating your subconscious mind. By speaking with others you are extending your reach and verifying. From this exercise, you may find an SMC you would never have thought of originally.

Trouble with Feedback: Meeting the big guy

Marty arrives at the office of the COO, Jack Wilson:

Marty: "Hi Mr. Wilson, thanks very much for meeting with me."

Jack: "You are welcome, and call me Jack."

Marty: "Thank you. I will. Several people in the company suggested that you would be the right person to speak with. I'm trying to find out why we don't obtain enough feedback on our products from our customers, and I've been told that there was a time when this wasn't the case. I thought you might know how we managed to obtain the feedback in the past, so we can improve the current situation."

Jack: "Yes, in the past the customers knew our products quite well, but things have changed. Now they know just enough to sell them and maybe sometimes not even that much. It is a definite problem…"

Marty: "Is there no way to obtain useful information from them relating to our products?"

Jack: "I wouldn't say that. Some of our customers know more than others, and we've tried to learn what we could from them. What we really need is to talk to the end-users. Our customers buy our products and display them in their stores and sell them, but they don't really use them. The ***real*** customers are those folks who use our appliances"

Marty: "So why don't we talk to them?"

Jack: "That's a good question. Do you know who they are and how to reach them? I sure don't."

Marty: "Isn't there a way to find out?"

Jack: "If you can find a way that would be great, but it sure isn't anything we've done before. Time is money. It may take a lot of digging, work, and legal agreements to obtain end user lists, let alone to communicate with these people."

Marty: (after a long pause) "That doesn't sound encouraging."

Jack: "Please, I don't mean to discourage you. If you can find a cost effective way to do this, the company will be all for it. Let me know if you come up with anything."

Marty now has a different view of the problem. There are still, however, no solutions that come to mind. The problem seems as intractable as ever. It should be noted, though, that Marty has now met with and cultivated an initial relationship with Jack, a strong potential SMC.

12
Intro to Stage 4 – Solve the BIP

Arrive at a solution by yourself or with limited outside help.

*(Or... Arrive at a solution with a group or team process, which is the focus of **Part 5: Group Dragonfly Thinking**)*

Coming to grips with the problem

It is now time to assemble all of the information and solve the problem. Solutions to BIPs often suggest themselves after you have gone over everything several times, or after you've taken a break and approached the problem anew. As a dragonfly circles over his pond and obtains a dragonfly's view of everything, so must you. When you do this, almost everything or at least everything that you have learned can be seen from afar. Most, if not all, of the pieces to the puzzle should be in view. But how do you assemble them? How do you come to the answer?

Moving forward

At this point, we have found a BIP, validated its importance, and interested an SMC in the process. We have essentially created a green light for a problem-solving process to begin. We must now move forward into the fourth stage – that of actually solving the problem, using all of the information and resources we've collected. This stage requires integrating the basics of dragonfly thinking (from Part 2) with the information gleaned in the process of formulating the problem in the workplace (from Part 3), and now bringing Dragonfly Thinking to the next stage: to specifically attacking a Big Important Problem, and solving it. **Part 4** of this book is all about that: it's an expansion of the problem-solving stage, and a detailed outline of what's involved in coming to a solution.

Part 4:

How to Solve Big, Important Problems

13

Mapping the landscape

Problems and Ponds

Although some dragonflies prefer cool running waters of spring-fed streams, lakes, or rivers, other dragonflies choose habitats in wetlands or marshes. Dragonflies do not choose polluted water, only intact ecosystems, and many types of dragonflies prefer the still waters of ponds.

A problem is not usually as simple as a pond that the dragonfly reigns over. A problem is often deceptive. It may not be what it seems to be. But is a pond really that simple, either? How many people know anything about ponds? The dragonfly knows.

The Pond in Spring and Summer

Dragonfly nymphs hatch from eggs, in the water or on water plants. The nymphs live in the water but leave after several stages: they crawl out on a plant stalk or twig, and then their skin splits and an adult dragonfly emerges.

Did you ever hear the expression: "a big fish in a small pond"? The dragonfly knows that a true pond has no fish. Fish eat larva, and in a small pond could eat all of them. A true pond is the best habitat for the dragonfly and many, many other life forms, in part because fish cannot live there. In the intense heat of summer, a true pond (aka, a *vernal pond*) dries up and becomes a mud hole – not a friendly place for a fish!

A true pond is actually filled with larvae, not fish. These larvae hatch from eggs and are part of the pond's food chain. In the summer, most of the inhabitants, now mature adults, crawl or hop away on land, or fly away through the air like the dragonfly. The pond becomes an evacuated city.

OVERSEER OF THE POND

The Pond in Fall and Winter

Later on, when the weather is cooler and the rains come, and the pond is again filled with water, the inhabitants return. Eggs are laid, and the cycle begins again. A true pond is a niche habitat for many types of plant and animal life. A pond is certainly not as simple as it seems.

The dragonfly discovered long ago that the pond is an ideal habitat, because despite its looks, it undergoes yearly cycles that make it inhospitable for predatory fish. Many types of problems that are encountered in the workplace or in life may appear also at first to be simple, but as you delve deeper, they are most certainly not. It is very important to study a problem, to explore it as you would a terrain, or as a dragonfly would explore the pond.

Remembering the deceptive simplicity of a pond, it is time to examine more closely how to solve a BIP.

14

Encountering obstacles

What is the chance of success of solving a new problem? This chance might *feel* like it's 100% when you first set out. You've just started a new journey, and the sky is the limit. If you plot your perceived probability of success versus time, you'll be starting out on top. Nothing stands in your way. That is, at least until you hit your first obstacle.

Say you are traveling on a road, and you screech to a halt in front of a big boulder. There is no choice but to engage this new obstacle if you are to eventually continue on down the road. This is usually not easy, and it can exact a psychological toll. It may seem that you are wasting time on a little detail instead of engaging the real problem, but in truth, solving BIPs often consists of identifying and facing many such small barriers.

If you can stay calm and analyze the boulder, you might see a way you can budge it a little. Perhaps there is a long tree branch lying on the ground that you can try to use as a lever. But the boulder is obstinate, and after you wedge the branch under it and heave, it snaps your branch and rolls back. Don't lose your steam. If you can keep up your spirits, you can go searching for a longer and thicker branch which can do the job. Once you manage to move the boulder off the road and drive past it, your probability of reaching your destination has jumped up.

As you continue driving down the road you will hit other obstacles. Perhaps a large bull is sitting in the middle of the road. Your chances of making it seem to sink once again. But you are now a bit more confident, and your feeling about your chances of success is a bit higher, so you get to work. You solve this obstacle, only to encounter another later on. Slowly, you move upward again, and so on, until eventually you have dealt with all of the obstacles and have solved the initial problem.

Probability of success vs. time

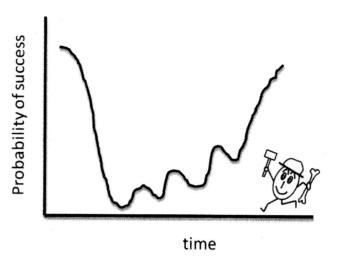

time

Did you notice a little man standing in the lower right corner of the success plot? That is Murphy. Engineers know Murphy quite well. When you embark on a big project or attempt to solve a big problem, it is an engineering folk legend that Murphy is hiding in there somewhere, ready to confound the whole process. This is also expressed in the form of *Murphy's Law.*

Murphy's Law: "If anything can go wrong, it will."

I have also heard of a theorem attributed to Murphy.

Murphy's Last Theorem: "If nothing has gone wrong, and things appear to be working, you are in for big trouble ahead."

Types of Obstacles

There are two basic types of obstacles that you may encounter. These may be called: *Regular* or *Common Obstacles* and *Fundamental Obstacles*. When an important problem is tackled, it is essential to make a list of all known obstacles. This list should be shared with every participant in the problem solving group or problem solving process. Sometimes not all of the obstacles are known until you start solving the problem. Typically, they are tied to the road you have taken, that is, to the particular type of approach to solving the initial problem.

Regular or Common Obstacles

Regular or Common Obstacles are the ones that you believe you can solve easily, like using a lever to move a big boulder that is blocking the road. These obstacles might take some effort to remove, but the way to do it is, at least in theory, clear.

Fundamental Obstacles

A Fundamental Obstacle is an obstacle that you cannot initially see any way to remove or to overcome. For example: suppose you are still driving as before, and the road suddenly splits ahead of you into the maw of an earthquake. You skid to a halt just in front of a steep gorge. Although the road continues beyond the gorge, you have no way to cross to the other side

Initially, you see no way to overcome this obstacle and to continue the journey. It is essential that the Fundamental Obstacles be written down and asterisked in the overall list of obstacles. Fundamental obstacles should be worked on first before anything else. This is essential, for if you are ever to put aside or abandon the problem solving effort, it is best to reach this conclusion before spending a lot of effort and time on surmountable obstacles even as insurmountable ones loom. Fundamental Obstacles are by far the most likely causes of project failure, and they are the challenges most in need of Dragonfly Thinking.

Fool's bootstrapping

Working on Regular or Common Obstacles before all of the Fundamental Obstacles have been removed is an extremely poor use of time and effort. A common pitfall is to work first on the simple obstacles, and only when such obstacles have been solved to then tackle the Fundamental ones. This type of prioritization is actually quite common, almost instinctive – to do the easy things first – and it generally wastes a lot of time.

If a fundamental obstacle has no workable solution the project should be put on hold. Alternatively, a Fundamental Obstacle may be solved and yet require a substantial change to the problem solving approach, thereby rendering obsolete the prior work on the easier Regular or Common Obstacles. This, in its worst case, may lead to a *fool's bootstrapping*, in which momentum that has been built towards the wrong solution becomes a sort of dogma or inertia, and itself becomes an obstacle to progress.

Trouble with Feedback: Glimpsing solutions

Marty and Briana are brainstorming ideas over lunch:

Marty: "Briana, I was thinking a lot about our lack of adequate feedback from our customers, and I was wondering if you ever thought of obtaining feedback on our products from our end users: the people who actually buy the products from our customers?"

Briana: "Sure I've thought about it, but we aren't really set up to do this."

Marty: "What would we need to do to set this up?"

Briana: "Well, if we sold our products online, we could conduct surveys and deal directly with the customer through customer service. But we don't sell online, and this isn't really possible without restructuring the whole company, I'd guess. Our products are displayed in show rooms in stores, and nobody would buy them sight unseen or even from a photograph over the internet."

Marty: "Could we develop some sort of online presence, even if it's not a sales shop?"

Briana: "We have a web site, as you know, but I don't see how this will really help for getting end users to give feedback. We don't really know who our end users are, and there's no incentive for them to contact us. Also, although many of our customers have online sales and product support capability, our products must be seen in show rooms and are never purchased sight unseen as with typical internet sales."

Marty: "What if we developed online capability to identify our end users?"

Briana: "It's possible, but why would the end users even bother going to our site?"

Marty: "What if we gave them something?"

Briana: "That's an idea, but they would have to go to our web site first, and they might not do that. Also, not all end users are computer savvy."

Marty: "I've been thinking about this, and it seems to me that our one potential shot is when they actually buy our product. Could we give them something when they buy our product if they send in a post card or go online or some such thing to sign up as an end user?"

Briana: "That might work; we could keep the communication options open so they could also call us. Like I said, not everyone is computer savvy."

Marty: "What could we give them that would make this work?"

Briana: "Well, our end users would probably like an extended warrantee. This would not cost us much, since our products are pretty robust anyway. Since it's something they wouldn't have to pay for, they might go for it. An added bonus is that it takes our customers – the stores – out of the loop as far as returns or service is concerned. They would actually like that, so there's an additional benefit."

Marty: "This could not happen overnight, though, could it? I'd expect there to be only a very gradual growth in the identified end user base over time. Everyone who elects to receive an extended warrantee would be in potential communication with us, but that would take a long time, many years or perhaps a decade, wouldn't it?"

Briana: "That's right, but even after a year we'd have an end user base large enough to obtain very important feedback from on our products. We could generate a good customer service impression and back it up. Then, I'd expect the end users to be loyal and helpful."

Marty: "Thank you so much, Briana. I'll put a plan together and run it by a few people. Let's discuss it again later in more detail."

Marty has persisted in his diligence in looking at the problem from all sides and has brainstormed a bit with Briana to come up with a possible solution. Unexpectedly, he and Briana may have come up with a solution that would work or possibly one that could be turned into one that would work.

Marty now has a lot more to do. Although he may be unaware of this, his actions have effectively set up an informal problem solving team consisting of the people he has been working with to understand the problem. His next step is to speak with John again, making sure to give a lot of the credit to Briana. After this, he will draw up a plan and meet Briana again, and he will meet again with his SMC, Mr. Wilson, that is: Jack.

15

Modes of thinking

A complex problem can usually be subdivided into a number of smaller problems. Overcoming key obstacles may require swooping down like the dragonfly to examine the obstacle and also to consider other parts of the overall problem. When you have identified the important parts of the problem, you can then brainstorm ideas, possibilities, and solutions to address each piece, and especially to tackle a key obstacle. To do this last part effectively, you must really sit down and *think*.

Traditional Models

There have been many studies conducted and books written about modes of thinking. In the 1950's psychologist J. P. Guilford developed the concept of "divergent thinking" as opposed to "convergent thinking".

Convergent thinking is what you do when you logically deduce the correct answers to simple problems, when there are a limited number of answers, such as in multiple choice tests, or when there is only one correct answer, such as in a math problem. It is the default type of thinking taught in most Western-fashioned schools. Correct answers are deduced through a logical process or by recalling previously learned facts. This is the type of thinking that is primarily measured by I.Q. (standing for 'Intelligence Quotient').

Convergent Thinking

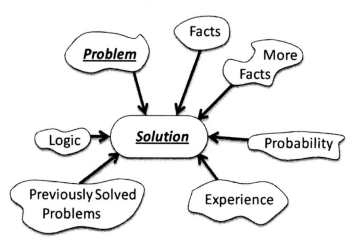

In contrast, divergent thinking is the generation of new possibilities. It is, in essence, creative, and not defined by logic. Nor is it measurable. Yet divergent thinking is essential for solving complex problems, problems for which high I.Q. alone cannot deduce solutions. Divergent thinking is an unbounded mode of thought. The divergent mode is considered to be creative, intuitive, imaginative, and innovative. There are no limiting rules or restrictions.

Divergent Thinking

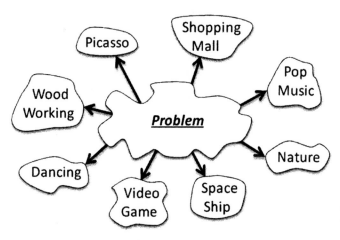

Another term called "lateral thinking" was originated by Edward de Bono in the mid-1960's (1967 book *New Think: The Use of Lateral Thinking*) and refers to solving problems by using an indirect, creative approach, and may be likened to outside of the box thinking.

Other kinds of thinking used for problem solving are described by David Lewis and James Greene in their 1982 book "Thinking Better". These authors refer to a "pathfinder strategy" (systematic to cover the ground very thoroughly) and a "helicopter strategy" (more random and at higher elevation to cover a lot of ground very quickly) for solving problems. They use as an example the problem of finding two lost children in a remote part of the country. You could miss the children with either strategy, but will usually find them more quickly with the helicopter strategy. If the children are in a forest or in a ravine covered by overhanging trees, however, the helicopter strategy my fail. The pathfinder strategy is typically more thorough but takes a lot longer to execute. Many other models for thinking have also been proposed.

All of these different models of thinking – convergent, divergent, lateral, pathfinder, etc. – are representations of actual thought processes. But it is important to remember that they are mere models, and they have their limitations in describing the holistic process of human thought. As in all of science, models are used to explain a system under study. But the model should never be confused with the system. It is only a representation, which highlights key features most salient to a given process. In truth, any physical phenomenon is far more complex.

Dragonfly thinking

Certainly, solving any complex problem will involve elements of both convergent and divergent thinking, as well as some others. The best problem solvers can use many modes in effective combination. As a dragonfly thinker, you can draw from the value of such models of thought, but it is also necessary to loosen your mind of them, for thought is a holistic and complicated process and perhaps cannot ever be truly characterized.

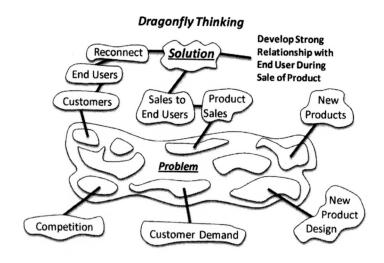

Dragonfly Thinking

As shown in the Dragonfly Diagram, Dragonfly Thinking is an umbrella method which pays homage to, but transcends, tight classifications such as *divergent* and *convergent* and *lateral*. It is a method and a mindset to view problems from wildly altered perspectives, enabling truly different solutions to problems encountered. It involves divergent thinking to come up with new possibilities plus convergent thinking to narrow down the field of possibilities when new information is obtained, plus many other forms of thinking, the whole complexity of the mental process, as appropriate.

More importantly, Dragonfly Thinking requires a mindset: that a problem is a terrain that can be mapped, even if at first it does not appear so.

Like the dragonfly flying over the pond, you can fly overhead to survey the terrain then swoop down to examine some feature in great detail. What is essential is to have faith that, by following the process and being persistent, you'll be able to map out the problem and ultimately come to a solution. As to *why* having faith and being persistent will work – that is the subject of the next chapter, and the basis of the Iceberg Principle.

16

Persistence, commitment, and *The Iceberg Principle of Epiphanies*

When you set out on a quest to solve a big problem, you must make it your own. You must wrestle with it, play with it, and carry it into different environments. You can even *sleep on it.* Sleeping on it is an often-heard phrase – why is this? Does sleeping on a problem actually work? The answer is *Yes!*

Some problems will stay with you if you are truly passionate about solving them. These problems will settle into your unconscious thoughts and even into your dreams. You may feel that this is bringing work home, and be turned off by the whole idea of it. Why bring work home? You would perhaps prefer to leave the work at the office during the 8 to 5 or whatever the hours may be and otherwise live a *real life* on the outside. If work isn't carefully partitioned, couldn't it become an all-consuming nightmare, swallowing your spare time, invading your freedom?

Actually, if you are having fun solving a problem, it is not work. It is rather like a crossword puzzle or a game of Sudoku – only it's not in front of you on a sheet of paper, it's embedded in your mind. You can work on the problem while you're driving. You can take the problem with you to the theater or to the baseball game and can ponder it between acts or innings or plays or during time outs. Alternatively, you could not even think about it but let your subconscious mind wrestle with it. This is why it is essential to choose a problem about which you can become passionate, and that has no time stress associated with it.

Remote thought triggers

A medical researcher friend of mine once told me that when he attends scientific conferences and listens to other scientists' talks, his thoughts wander to his own research and his own problems, and that often then and there is when he gets his best ideas. He relayed to me that thoughts of his own research and new approaches to dealing with his most intractable problems are often triggered when he views other scientists' slides, even though the slides and the talks typically deal with an entirely different subject from his own. I've also had similar experiences. Many great thinkers report that they have received great ideas in dreams, often in response to an important problem they have been working on. Archimedes, even, discovered the principle of density while he was daydreaming in the bath. This phenomenon, it appears, is quite widespread.

A classic story of a dream aiding problem solving in the field of science is the story of the German Chemist, August Kekule. He was trying to picture the structures of certain molecules, at the time thought of as chains of atoms bonded together. He sought the correct structure in order to help understand the properties of these molecules.

One evening in 1865, Kekule fell asleep in front of his fireplace. In his dreams, he saw snakes dancing. When one snake grabbed his tail in his mouth and formed a ring, Kekule woke up and realized that the molecules, until then thought of as chains of atoms like beads on a string, could also have a ring structure: like a necklace. This realization forever changed the field of chemistry. This famous dream of the *benzene ring* of carbon molecules helped lay the groundwork for many of the great discoveries of the Twentieth Century.

This kind of instant insight is by no means confined to science. Stephen King, the American bestselling author of horror, suspense, science fiction, and fantasy novels, and who has had many movies, short films, and television shows based on his works, is also known for his book: "On Writing, A Memoir of the Craft" (Copyright 2000, Scribner paperback 2010). This short autobiography and guide for writers is considered by many to be his finest work. In this book, King teaches the craft of writing and reveals his trials, tribulations, and experiences as a writer. In one portion of the book, he describes a flash of creative insight that enabled him to finish "The Stand", a novel that many consider his best fiction work. He describes how, after weeks of boredom and non-productivity, he had taken to going for long walks to let his mind wander. On one of these walks he gained a sudden insight, which he describes like this:

"It arrived whole and complete – gift wrapped, you could say – in a single bright flash... At one moment I had none of this; at the next I had all of it."

So where does this all lead us?

The Iceberg Principle of Epiphanies

Dr. Oliver Sacks, a famous British neurologist, has studied the mind extensively, deriving great insights from patients with a variety of mental disorders as well as with unusual mental abilities. Sacks has written many books and articles about his studies and experiences. His famous book "Awakenings" was the basis for the 1990 feature film of the same name – a film starring Robert De Niro and Robin Williams – a wonderful and deeply moving film that describes the experiences of Dr. Sacks (Williams) and how a new drug (L-Dopa) successfully awakened many patients from catatonic states that had lasted as long as 30 years.

Dr. Sacks was the keynote speaker at a conference I attended. He told the story of the scientist Mendeleev who, after years of study of the chemical elements, in a vivid dream, conceived all at once of the periodic table of the elements. Mendeleev quickly scribbled it on the back of an envelope. Following this was a description of the mathematician Poincare, who while embarking on a geologic trip, suddenly realized that the equations he was manipulating in order to solve a problem in algebra were identical in form to those which characterize non-Euclidean geometry. It was not a problem he had been working on, and the realization arrived to him fully formed.

Sacks then recounted another such revelation experienced by the composer Berlioz, who had a dream where a new and breathtakingly beautiful symphony unfolded. In this case, however, Berlioz was unable to act upon it, because he had to do other work upon awakening to pay the bills to support his family. By the time he got back to the subject of his dream he had forgotten too much, and the new symphony was lost.

As I listened to these stories from Oliver Sacks, who in my view was giving them new meaning and new context, I too experienced an epiphany relating to a familiar phenomenon that I had been amusing myself with for at least a year. I came away thinking that my phenomenon-related revelation was somehow connected to the phenomenon underlying the stories described by Dr. Sacks and perhaps might shed insight upon them. Yet, these two phenomena appeared totally different to me, and were it not for this sudden insight, or rather the euphoria that I experienced in that moment, I never would have connected them.

Immediately afterward I described my new insight to some friends who also were present at Dr. Sacks talk. They liked it. The following day, I described it to Dr. Sacks himself after his scheduled morning talk. I believe he liked it too. I will provide more detail here and leave it to the reader to judge whether there is any deep insight into human thought in my reasoning.

For about a year I had been acutely aware of a phenomenon that I shall call "the small world phenomenon". This awareness had been reinforced by how often friends would tell me they met someone on a cruise or on an airplane or by chance, say in a foreign country, and it turned out that the person they met was actually a distant relative, or was married to a distant relative, or lived on the same block when they were children, or some other such coincidence. They would follow the vignette with: "It's a small world". This is also similar to Carl Jung's idea of *synchronicity*.

When I heard these "It's a small world" stories, I often wondered what would have happened if these coincidences hadn't happened because the timing wasn't exactly correct, if the paths missed by a few seconds. I visualized one person turning down a corridor just as another – his or her long lost relative – emerged, and the two of them failing to see each other or meet. I called this a "near miss". I also found it significant that none of these coincidences would have been manifest if the two people met but failed to speak (lack of communication or perhaps lack of connectivity). If there was no communication, the nature of their hidden relationship would then not have been revealed, **despite the fact that it was still there**. I thought of the coincidences associated with the "small world phenomenon" as **the tip of the iceberg**: that is, the portion that is visible.

The near misses of such encounters are not visible, and in effect are not perceived, yet there are probably so very many more of them than there are actual encounters. These near misses are like the part of an iceberg that's under water. (Thinking of the "entire" iceberg may make the world seem conceptually "even smaller".) Now, while listening to Dr. Sacks discuss the sudden deep insights of Mendeleev, Poincare, and Berlioz, **the iceberg and the small world phenomenon flew into my mind**. It was not merely a distracting thought but one that I felt to be of deep significance, as though I had solved a problem I had been wrestling with. But what was it? How did the iceberg relate to what Sacks was describing?

A few moments later I knew the answer. *It was that the unconscious mind is always working, but it is like the submerged portion of the iceberg. There are an inordinate number of near misses and failures relative to the achievement of appropriate connectivity between mentally held concepts, perhaps circulating in the brain. When something connects and resolves, it is sent to the conscious mind, and a new thought occurs. The conscious mind may be thought of as the visible part of the iceberg.*

Our thoughts and memories are *graded* by emotional and

other content, so unlike the bytes of a digital computer, they have associated with them varying degrees of significance. For a thought that resolves a long-standing problem that you have been arduously working on or a thought that uncovers a personal relationship that you were not aware of, the grading associated with the new thought is that much stronger. A thought with a high significance grading, transmitted from the unconscious to the conscious mind, may well be strong enough to be remembered from a dream. I call this a natural consequence of the *"Iceberg Theory".*

The human nervous system is highly complex. In the brain there are at least 10 billion nerve cells or neurons, each with thousands of *synapses,* or connections to communication cables leading to other nerve cells – as many as 10,000 synapses for some neurons. Nerve cells transmit electrical signals, called action potentials, to other nerve cells, and considering the possible number of combinations of neurons signals at any one moment, the number of possible phone calls between neurons is apparently greater than the number of all of the atoms of ordinary matter in the visible universe!

Most brain activity is unconscious, like the *portion of the iceberg that is under water.* Perhaps we are thinking nearly all of the time but are not conscious of it. Perhaps also, when two thoughts with a "high grading" have a combined significance, like two distant relatives unexpectedly meeting each other, the conscious mind then becomes aware of it. If so, there may very well be an enormous preponderance of near misses in the vast and complex brain, in which the two distant relatives do not meet.

An iceberg theory of human conscious and unconscious processes might explain the phenomena described by Dr. Oliver

Sacks: the development of a unifying thought in chemistry; the sudden solution of a long standing mathematical problem; the birth of deep seeded creative insight of a purely abstract nature; or the creation of a unique musical composition.

So what is the key point? How do we turn the iceberg theory into action? It's actually simple. As we've seen in the cases of Mendeleev, Poincare, and Berlioz, ***bringing a problem everywhere with you will vastly increase the chance of connecting the hidden dots.*** You never know what kind of environment will provide the missing link for your solution. If you treat the problem like an interesting puzzle, and keep it in mind while you're driving, eating, sitting, walking, and sleeping, you never know when a totally novel solution might materialize. You do not have to think about it continuously, only deeply enough and often enough to engage your subconscious mind, which will do the heavy lifting.

GENERAL PRINCIPLE C, *The Iceberg Principle of Epiphanies*:
By bringing a problem everywhere with you, you will vastly increase the chance of connecting the hidden dots, and finding a solution.

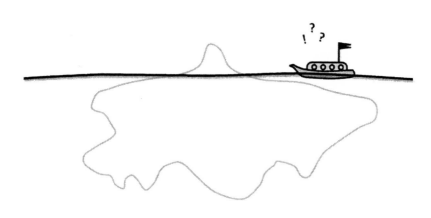

ICEBERG THEORY

17

Stage 4 – Solve the BIP

We have now explored many elements of Dragonfly Thinking. We are ready to go into the mechanics of solving BIP's – to return to Stage 4 from the end of Part 3 of this book.

The method that follows outlines a specific set of tactics for solving your BIP, once you've chosen it. A problem that really counts is best: a problem or issue with an "A rating." If practiced, this method can become very effective. It can also be performed with many times the vision and power by a group, as will be seen later (for example, to tackle big company problems). As you will see, if you can learn to orchestrate or lead a group, you'll move mountains.

TACTICAL PROCESS 4:
An eight-step process for problem solving

The following 8-step Tactical Process will enable you to master the art of problem solving. This is the fundamental process for taking what you've learned about Dragonfly Thinking and applying it practically to your BIP.

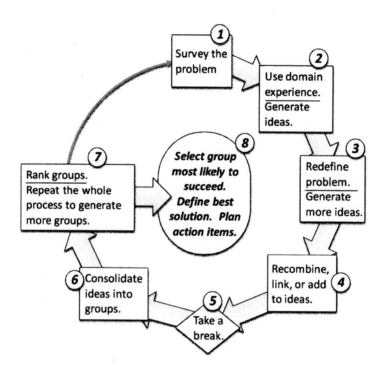

1. Survey the problem
2. Use domain experience. Generate ideas.
3. Redefine problem. Generate more ideas.
4. Recombine, link, or add to ideas.
5. Take a break.
6. Consolidate ideas into groups.
7. Rank groups. Repeat the whole process to generate more groups.
8. Select group most likely to succeed. Define best solution. Plan action items.

SOLO PROBLEM SOLVING: EIGHT STEPS

Eight steps for cultivating the ability to use dragonfly thinking for solo problem solving are:

1. **Survey the problem from different vantage points, like the dragonfly**

    Consider any difficult task or problem as a challenge with many solutions. Look at the problem from above, as though you were flying over it. Phrase the problem as: how can I do such and such? Or: how can we do such and such? For example:

    > *"How can I impress Apple Computers sufficiently to obtain a contract worth 10 million dollars?"*
    > With this statement of the problem you can proceed according to the next steps. It is also important, however, to swoop down and consider breaking the problem into component parts and reformulating it to consider each part independently. For example, the first part might be: *"What other business transactions may be possible with Apple and our Company?"* You can construct several of these different views of the larger picture of the entire "pond" of doing business with Apple.

2. **Use domain experience & generate new ideas**

    It is important to know the domain associated with the problem; i.e., to have *domain experience*. If the problem deals with a particular customer, you should know the customer and the customer's business. If you do not know much about the customer, you should either do your due diligence, or work on a different problem.

    If you have acquired sufficient domain experience or at least sufficient domain knowledge, write down as many potential solutions as you can think of, no matter how ridiculous they may be. Quantity is what's important here, not quality. Don't let your experience limit your idea generation. Continue to observe the problem from different vantage points. This is the essence of Dragonfly Thinking.

    > *We can show them how good our robotic nanotechnology circuit design system is.*
    > *We can provide a list of endorsements from our clients.*
    > *We can discuss our recent growth spurt.*

> *We can showcase the way we used venture capital funding to develop our business and reach positive cash flow.*
> *We can emphasize our community and charity work.*
> ...

3. **Redefine the problem & generate more ideas accordingly**

   After the first round of brainstorming, it might make sense to redefine the problem in order to focus ideas towards more helpful areas. Again, seek different vantage points for idea generation. This might be clearer to you now that you've thought of some initial ideas. For example:

   > *How can we show Apple that we understand their business objectives and can help?*
   > **We can run numbers on their public financials, and appeal to the parts of their business that could benefit from our products.*
   > **We can interview people we know who used to be in their company to better understand their culture.*
   > **We can put ourselves in the shoes of their customers to better understand the kinds of challenges they face and how we can help.*
   > ...

4. **Recombine, link, or add to ideas**

   Up until now, you have been thinking up as many ideas as possible, with minimal value judgements. The next step is to take a look at these ideas, and determine which ones group together or can be combined. This is a *convergent* rather than *divergent thinking process.* Add or link onto an existing idea to create another solution, still retaining the original. For example:

   > *We can talk about how we operate in a situation that demonstrates our understanding of the challenges they face, or in a situation that they have not yet seen but our other customers have, etc.*

5. **Take a break.**
   This step is critical, as it relates to the *Iceberg Principle*, and will allow your mind to mull over the process subconsciously. It is often where the best ideas come from. Taking breaks is a powerful device for any problem solving endeavor, as long as you have intense problem solving and thinking sessions you are taking breaks from (if you never develop the discipline to sit down for uninterrupted time and very deliberately *think* about a problem, a break won't do you any good).

6. **Consolidate ideas into groups based on similarity**
   Come back and examine the list of possible (including some impossible) ideas or solutions. Consolidate or group similar solutions, which may be thought of as terrain sectors.
   Set A of solutions
   Set B of solutions
   Set C of solutions

7. **Rank groups and repeat process**
   Make a list of the consolidated solutions, giving each group a name. View this list from above. Once again, go into dragonfly mode and seek different vantage points. Decide which group is most likely to succeed. For example:
   Impressing them.
   Demonstrating how our approach will generate exciting new products for them.
   Showing we understand them.
   Demonstrating we have dealt with similar situations.
   Showing them we are great.
   ...
   Now repeat the process using alternative component parts of the problem from step 1 or different reformulations of the same problem from step 1. When you have finished, you'll have additional groups, akin to the groups immediately above.

8. **Select the most likely group, and work towards solution**

   Select the group most likely to succeed and begin developing action items to implement a plan. For example:

   Apple would be most receptive if we demonstrate that we understand their culture and product objectives and could make more money for them. We need to execute the following steps to demonstrate this: Step 1......; Step 2.......; Step 3.......; etc. When they indicate they would like our help, we should do the following: Step 1...: Step 2...; Step 3....; etc.

As long as you can generate new groups it is important to continue with Steps 1 through 7. By selecting the best "group" of ideas you are consolidating ideas. These grouped ideas can be restated as a concept or approach to the problem or task at hand. By attacking a problem in this way, you'll tend to avoid many of the pitfalls of being trapped by our brains, senses, or the environmental norms of the workplace. Steps 1-4 enable free flow of ideas, and then steps 6-8 help to select or discriminate among the best options. This is much better than forcing constraints upon the generation of the ideas or approaches in the first place. *It is extremely important to be free of any constraints when generating ideas!*

After implementing all eight steps, you can then take another break and then go back and repeat the entire process once again, or even twice, trying to visualize the problem anew and perhaps ultimately deriving an entirely different solution. You can either combine the solutions or, alternatively, you can simply move forward with the best solution from the different brainstorming sessions. Although it may seem repetitive, if you develop the discipline to allow free flow of ideas, taking appropriate breaks to revisit the problem anew, you will harnesses the enormous power of the subconscious mind, and you will discover new avenues and approaches that were not visible before. Sometimes it is best to put the problem aside for a day or two before attacking it again. This rest period will empower the subconscious mind and enable Dragonfly Thinking.

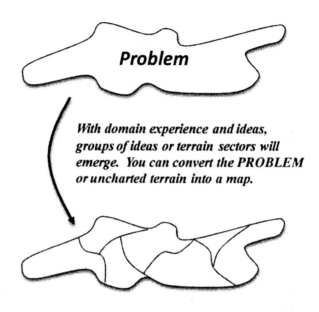

Problem

With domain experience and ideas, groups of ideas or terrain sectors will emerge. You can convert the PROBLEM or uncharted terrain into a map.

EXERCISE 4: Try the 8-step process on a brainteaser

You can do this exercise with the brainteaser below, or feel free to use one from another source. The point of the exercise is to solve the brainteaser by deliberately following the Eight steps for Solo Problem Solving. It is important that you do each step in turn, so you get a feel for the whole problem solving process.

The Great Diamond Robbery

A crafty criminal was being chased by the police. He was carrying a small sack of diamonds that he had just stolen from a diamond dealer. He ran past a street corner where two little boys were

*selling lemonade. There were three large pitchers of lemonade
and a stack of cups. The sign read: "Lemonade for Sale 15 Cents
per Cup," and a smaller sign read: "All Proceeds will be used for
our School Science Project". In a flash, the criminal dropped all of
the diamonds into an opened ice chest that the boys were using.
The diamonds were completely lost in the ice and could not be
seen. Two policemen arrived seconds later and apprehended the
criminal but could not locate the diamonds. One of the policemen
asked the boys if they had seen any diamonds. Without saying a
word, within 10 seconds one of the boys handed the policeman
a whole bunch of diamonds, separated from the ice. How did he
do this, and what was the school science project probably about?*

Once again, the steps are:

1. **Survey the problem from different vantage points,
   like the dragonfly** (i.e., read the brainteaser, and make
   sure you understand what it's asking)
2. **Use domain experience & generate new ideas** (i.e.,
   think of as many ideas as possible)
3. **Redefine the problem & generate more ideas
   accordingly** (i.e., think if the problem can be redefined,
   now that you've delved into it more)
4. Recombine, link, or add to ideas.
5. Take a break.
6. Consolidate ideas into groups based on similarity.
7. Rank groups and repeat the process.
8. Select the most likely group, and work towards a
   solution.

Convert to action items or in this case to an "aha" solution to
the brainteaser. A solution for the diamond robbery brainteaser
is provided in the 'additional brainteasers' appendix.

18

Exercise and relaxation – keys to problem solving

Creativity has been shown to be enhanced by exercise in several scientific studies: notably, by Steinberg, Sykes, and Moss, et al in the British Journal of Sports Medicine 1997; 31: 240-245, where 63 subjects were studied, and three measures were used to assess creativity changes. Conversely, stress will reduce creativity and probably also intelligence on a temporary basis, and extreme anxiety or fear may reduce it further or abolish it, since a fight or flight response could promote reflexive behavior in place of thinking skills.

Physical exercise energizes the body and the mind. The value of physical exercise on the many systems of the body, including the cardiovascular system and nervous system is continually being realized, researched, and written about. Aside from increasing health and lifespan, exercise also leads to relaxation and facilitates problem solving and especially Dragonfly Thinking. Sleeping after a good physical workout puts the body and mind in a relaxed state, and helps solutions materialize from the bottom of the iceberg.

Building and transcending schemas

An interesting example of sleeping on problems is in rock climbing. One popular form of rock climbing, called *bouldering*, involves solving climbing *problems* without a rope but using hands and feet, only, on actual boulders or in an artificial rock gym. Rarely does a boulderer go more than 10 or 15 feet off the ground – and safety mats are used below to cushion a possible fall – but the sheer mental and physical challenge is immense and inspires bouldering competitions all over the world.

Boulderers often speak of bouldering problems as similar to logic problems, only different in that they involve not only the mind but the whole body. Subtle changes in body position or grip could make the difference between attaining the top of a boulder versus falling off, and the margins for success can be miniscule. It appears that muscle memory can synergize with the problem solving capability of the mind in sleep, and when a climber tackles a very difficult bouldering problem and doesn't solve it, often sleeping on it will allow the unconscious mind to sort out the solution. It is common for boulderers to struggle for many hours on a boulder problem, unable to find the solution, but then the next day, after a good night's rest, to come back and finish it easily. It is not a matter of strength, but of ingrained muscle memory which was fully integrated and primed during sleep.

A classic book on rock climbing is "The Rock Warrior's Way, Mental Training for Climbers" by Arno Ilgner. In the start of the 2003 edition of this book, Ilgner says: "An important component of our consciousness is our habitual system of beliefs and motivation. Our early learning – our socialization into our culture – has determined much of our mental structure that subdues our potential."

In this book, special *memories* are described which sports physiologists call *schemas*. Schemas are physical movements that have become incorporated into an automatic cache, so that executing the particular move becomes instinctive under the right circumstances. Pole vaulters, for instance, develop schemas for their jumps, so that when they vault off the ground, their bodies automatically know how to respond given a particular height and intensity with which they launched off. These schemas, which all athletes train to condition, exist partly in the brain and partly in the nerves and fibers of the muscles used in a sport. Schemas are critical to success, but they can also serve as a comfort zone that is difficult to break out of, if we are not in the habit of continually updating and incorporating more schemas. In his book, Ilgner refers to the ego as: "....a mental construct, produced by socialization, which rewards and punishes us with feelings of self-worth."

In climbing, the ego is a kind of a box, and abandoning the ego is like thinking outside of the box. Physically and mentally, rock climbers are trapped within schemas, and new challenges they face that fall outside their schemas can seem daunting or impossible. The objective is to employ relaxation, proper posture, and breathing – even relaxing facial muscles – to achieve a complete unity of body and mind for success in solving the problem and achieving a successful climb. New challenges can be overcome, and new schemas learned, but only with the right approach and attitude.

Relaxation

The take home lesson is that if you embrace a problem and relax, you can amass the powerful mental ability to come to grips with and solve it. If you can relax, you can even have fun during the problem solving process. It might even become a great way to pass the time, and in the end you can experience a profound sense of fulfillment when you arrive at a solution. Success requires a special type of discipline. This is the discipline and willingness to stand *stuck* in the face of difficult obstacles, and to feel okay, even exhilarated, with that feeling of *stuckness.*

A good problem solver will keep probing and thinking while stuck, until some new insight emerges. *Stuckness* feels interesting, not daunting or terrifying. And this is, incidentally, why stress is often bad for true problem solving – if we are impatient, the feeling of being *stuck* can quickly turn foul, and we will try to rush out of it when we are not ready. This is true not only in climbing and other sports, but in problem solving in general. We must stay relaxed if we are to stay limber and supple while stuck, and ultimately to piece out a new way of viewing our obstacle.

There are many relaxation techniques to focus the mind and body while you are awake, including doing exercise such as distance running. Some distance runners claim that they get their best ideas while running. Stephen King preferred long walks. For relaxation as well as exercise, yoga, meditation, and moving meditations of various types, such as Tai Chi, may be effective. Perhaps the ultimate relaxation technique is a good night's sleep. A relaxed mind and a relaxed body are critical assets to nourish when solving a difficult problem. ***Do not underestimate the importance of physical exercise and relaxation.***

It is important to recognize that when you are solving a BIP you may become stuck. You may not be able to advance or see a clear path to a solution. There is nothing wrong with this. In fact, being stuck is often part of the process. If you are stuck, put the problem aside, but do not abandon it. Try to relax in the best way you know how. A new approach may appear when you least expect it, and especially if you are carrying the problem into many different environments in your subconscious mind.

You are well on your way when you have validated that the problem you have selected is important and that solving it will be of great benefit. Others will definitely take notice if you solve it. An effective solution to a BIP may be an important contribution to your organization, business, or to society. Keep this in mind, as well.

19
Persistence, Engagement, and New Ideas

Suppose you have your list of problems, possibly including at least one Big Important Problem (BIP). As we've discussed, this list can be narrowed down to one problem that you wish to work on. Say that you have already selected the problem of choice and have also selected a mentor to validate that this problem is real and important. Perhaps you have already thought a lot about the problem, but you currently are out of ideas. You see no idea how to find a solution: you're at an impasse. Where do new ideas come from? How will you find them? How will you be able to propel yourself outside of your schemas, and into a successful solution to the problem you have chosen to work on?

The answer, surprisingly, is that new ideas can be triggered from anywhere. This is the essence of the iceberg principle, explained earlier, and a key element of effective Dragonfly Thinking. The important issue is not *what you are looking at* in order to generate ideas, but rather *what kind of mindset you bring with you*. If you are constantly primed with your question – juggling it, kneading it, stretching and squashing it, feeling it over for any possible weaknesses – you might find the answer in the ocean, having your teeth cleaned at the dentist, making coffee, or reading a book.

Or maybe it's the *structure* of the dentist's office, the way the dental hygienists *relate* to each other, the very *feel* of the place that will suddenly reveal your solution. The key is *your mindset*, not the specific details of your surroundings. Inspiration can be triggered by anything. There is enough *stuff* around to be picked and chosen from that, likely enough, *something* will eventually connect in your mind, and will manifest an idea for a solution. But that is only *if* you keep the concepts broiling about in your mind. In order to come up with novel ideas, you must be deeply engaged in your problem, actually carrying it with you through many types of experiences in your day, while you allow your unconscious mind to really work with it. This is a critical task for doing Dragonfly Thinking.

GENERAL PRINCIPLE D: New ideas can come from anywhere.

Where do new ideas come from that can help you solve the problem you are working on? Guess what? Once again, they can come from anywhere. You must be engaged; you must be receptive; you must be in the process of coming to grips with the problem, wrestling with it, considering it from all aspects and angles and nuances, especially from a distant or aerial perspective. And, you must be relaxed, or you may not be as receptive as you could be. The ideas will emerge. You'll see. They will materialize when the conditions are right, and they'll lead to successful solutions to the most difficult problems.

Flash Case Study: Flower Pot

One morning while I was working in my first job at a laboratory instrument company, I was trying to set up a flow of liquid that could be easily varied according to a set pattern. I wasn't sure of the best way to do this, especially since I wanted to keep the solution simple. In the afternoon, as I was looking at a flower pot, the problem I was working on suddenly flew into my mind. Why did this happen? How could this flower pot be of help? What clue did it provide? Rather than ignore the correlation between the flower pot and the problem, I sought a connection. It didn't take long. The flower pot is a container with a hole in the bottom, and I realized that I could solve my problem using a tank with a bottom outlet, where the flow of liquid would be greater when the tank was full but would gradually diminish: exactly the solution we needed.

The important consideration is to look at a problem from many angles, vantages, and perspectives. As you fly about the problem terrain like a dragonfly, you must come down periodically for a closer look at things when you think you may have identified something that will help. To employ your thinking skills, especially the creative aspects, you must be relaxed. Often, when you least expect it, a great idea will present itself.

The Medici Effect

Frans Johansson observed that the intersection of fields, disciplines, and cultures enables merging of existing concepts into a large number of extraordinary ideas. He named this phenomenon the "Medici Effect", after the banking family in Fifteenth-century Florence Italy. The Medici family funded artists and innovators in a broad range of disciplines, which contributed to a remarkable burst of creativity that became known as the Renaissance. This is still considered one of the most innovative eras in recorded history.

In his book by the same name (*The Medici Effect*, 2006 Harvard Business School Press) Johansson delves deeply into combinations of disciplines and cultures leading to an explosion of new ideas and innovation. He advocates establishing networks with people in your own field, but then breaking away from those networks in order to create intersections with different fields and to cross-fertilize ideas. As both a long-term career path and as a short-term approach to attacking a single problem, this cross-fertilization by experiencing different fields can be the single most important fuel for innovation.

Mixing and Congealing Ideas

In an OP ED in the New York Times on August 4, 2010, Thomas L. Friedman, author of "The World is Flat" (2005; Farrar, Straus & Giroux) quoted from an essay he had read on creativity: "To be creative requires divergent thinking (generating many unique ideas) and then convergent thinking (combining those ideas into the best result)." Friedman continued: "And where does divergent thinking come from? It comes from being exposed to divergent ideas and cultures and intellectual disciplines." He then quoted Marc Tucker, president of the National Center on Education and the Economy: "One thing we know about creativity is that it typically occurs when people who have mastered two or more quite different fields use the framework in one to think afresh about the other. Intuitively you know this is true. Leonardo da Vinci was a great artist, scientist, and inventor, and each specialty nourished the other. He was a great lateral thinker. But if you spend your whole life in one silo, you will never have either the knowledge or mental agility to do the synthesis, connect the dots, which is usually where the next great breakthrough is found."

Friedman also commented on what is in his view America's most important competitive advantage: "the sheer creative energy that comes when you mix all our diverse people and cultures together: We live in an age when the most valuable asset any economy can have is the ability to be creative – to spark and imagine new ideas, be they Broadway tunes, great books, cancer drugs..."

Trouble with Feedback: SMC influence

Marty and Jack, the SMC, are meeting in Jack's office:

Marty: "Thanks for meeting with me, Jack."

Jack: "You're welcome. What's on your mind?"

Marty: "I think we have a possible approach to the problem of obtaining feedback on our products directly from the end users – our 'real customers.'"

Jack: "How so?"

Marty: "At the point of sale, we have an opportunity to get contact information from end users. If we act on this – especially if we give them something – we might be able to connect with them. For example, we could ask them to fill out a form with feedback on the product they bought and have now used."

Jack: "What would we give them?"

Marty: "How about an extended warrantee?"

Jack: "Hmm, that's an interesting thought. We could look into this possibility quite easily." (Jack picks up the phone briefly, and Joe walks into Jack's office.)

Jack: "Joe, meet Marty! He is from the Publications Department and has a plan that Marketing may like, which involves offering an extended warrantee to customers. Marty, meet Joe! He is a financial guy and also an implementer of new procedures. He's your guy for figuring out if this idea will be workable."

Joe: "I'll get right onto it. Marty, would you like to come to my office?"

Jack: "Let's see what happens. Good luck!"

Marty and Joe go to Joe's office, and continue:

Joe: "I thought it would be good to spend a few minutes in my office first. Jack is very busy right now. Have you met with anyone in Marketing?"

Marty: "Yes. I met with Briana in Sales and also with John and Cecilia."

Joe: "Have you met with Maria or with any of the Manufacturing people, yet?"

Marty: "No. Maria is the new VP of Marketing and Sales, isn't she?"

Joe: "That's right. You'll like her. She's very open to new ideas. We should probably meet with her first and then meet with the Manufacturing and Product Support people. I'll arrange it."

A little bit later, Joe from Finance is introducing Marty to Maria, the VP of Marketing and Sales:

Joe: "Hi Maria. This is Marty from Publications. He came up with an idea to connect us with end users so we can get direct marketing information on our products. Marty, maybe you can explain it?"

Marty: "Nice to meet you, Maria. Brianna from Sales and I have this idea of developing a relationship with end users when they buy our products. We thought that if we give them something, like an extended warrantee, they might be willing to fill out a form after they use our product and also provide their contact information for future use."

Maria: "I like that. I like that a lot. It also opens up all sorts of possibilities for future marketing initiatives. Maybe the extended warrantee won't be enough and could be costly.

Joe: "That's right, but we can find out easily. I have a meeting scheduled with Manufacturing."

Maria: "Maybe a cash rebate could work, too. We could also extend the warrantee on the product. Joe, could you work out the numbers on this?"

Joe: "Sure!"

CASE STUDY II: Felix's tools

Sometimes a big, important problem is assigned to you or you find yourself assigned to working on a team to solve it. This case study deals with a problem I was once assigned in my work, and that I will always remember.

In my first industrial job, I worked for a company as a biomedical engineer in the Advanced Development Department. The company I worked for made analytical equipment used in laboratories. After only two weeks with the company, I was assigned to a project with two other employees. This project was all about solving an important technical problem. At the time, an advanced prototype product, an analytical instrument, was not functioning as it should, and it was not clear why this was happening. This late stage prototype product had undergone its development cycle in my department and had then been sent to the Product Engineering Department, where a problem was discovered that apparently had escaped detection earlier. The problem was sporadic but serious. Only when certain samples to be analyzed were introduced to the instrument did the problem occur, causing the system to malfunction. It was important to solve this problem so the product could be finalized, manufactured, and sold, and it was costing the company a lot of time and money each day that this product was delayed.

My group, consisting of three individuals, was not the only group assigned to this problem. Since it was a very serious issue for the company, there were a number of other small groups in the Product Engineering Department also working furiously on it, trying a number of different approaches. My group was assigned to the project by my boss. My boss's boss, who had approved release of the instrument, felt responsible for the delay and was coordinating our efforts with the other small groups in the Product Engineering Department, where the product had been transferred prior to manufacturing and where the problem had first been discovered. Product Engineering had been attempting to solve this problem for several weeks already, with no success.

The team I was assigned to consisted of me and two other individuals: Don and Felix. Don was a senior systems engineer and was one of the few people I've ever met who could merely glance at a complex electronic circuit diagram on paper and instinctively know what the electronics were supposed to do, and even whether there was a design flaw. Felix, a senior electronics technician, could build almost anything electronic. He was assigned only part time to this project, since he had other work to finish. Don was a comprehensive thinker and problem solver with a lot of industrial experience, mostly learned in previous employment in the defense industry. He believed that the problem in the advanced prototype instrument had to do with fluid flow and not electronics, although some others disagreed. In fact, there were many opinions floating around as to what was responsible for the difficulty with this new instrument. The instrument probably had the equivalent of hundreds of feet of wire in its coils and circuitry, but perhaps only ten feet or so of tubing. A liquid sample entered the tubing by suction, flowed forward through a few coils, received additions of special analytical reagents via side connections, underwent chemical reactions, and eventually flowed into the analysis chamber where an intense light beam penetrated the processed sample. The diffracted light was then detected and analyzed via specialized electronic circuitry, giving an accurate chemical analysis of the sample.

The actual problem was that a sample with high concentration of a particular substance would occasionally come along and contaminate the several samples that came before or after it. This wasn't supposed to happen, since the tubing through which the samples flowed isolated the samples effectively and maintained sample integrity. There were many tests carried out in Product Engineering on the tubing to illustrate that the tubing worked properly. Don had friends in Product Engineering and knew exactly what was going on, so he suspected that the tubing itself was not the problem. Instead, he thought that one of the many connections or fittings at different points along the length of the tubing was the culprit. Perhaps, something was mixing or stalling where a reagent entered the sample stream, or where something was removed from the sample stream. As a result, Don kept looking at me, the default fluid dynamics person, for insight into how to solve the problem. Don said: "You are the fluid dynamics guy. You should be able to figure out what's going wrong in the fluid flow path."

Don and I had intense brainstorming sessions. Meanwhile, Felix was nearby building his electronic circuits on breadboards used for testing related to other projects. If we needed him, Felix was there and ready, but it was not exactly clear yet how he might help. Felix occasionally hummed a tune as he worked, and he seemed to enjoy every minute of his labors. As Don and I continued our analysis of the malfunctioning instrument and as we thought we had narrowed the problem down to a particular area, something caught my attention. I noticed occasionally that Felix would stop humming his tune and become annoyed. I looked more closely and saw that his annoyance always cropped up after he tested his circuitry, and saw that it was not performing properly. I noted that during a test, Felix would attach his Volt-Ohm-Meter or his oscilloscope with swift hands and determination, and look at the readouts to learn how the electronic circuits were functioning. If a circuit required modification or needed to be fixed, he would attend to it. Then, after a time, he would be humming his tunes again and would happily pick up his soldering iron or soldering gun and fix the problem in the electronic circuit.

It was in that moment of observation that I had an epiphany. All at once, an idea flew into my mind. Now, if I had not been immersed in intense sessions with Don trying to solve a problem for my company, Felix's actions would probably not have had any special significance. But I was immersed in what was for me at that time a *Big* problem, and recalling reticular activation and the iceberg principle, it is easy to see why my brain was tuned to be receptive to just about anything that might help. *The revelation was that Felix had tools!* Don and I didn't! In an instant, I thought like a dragonfly! Flying at a high altitude, I saw the landscape, the scenario, from afar. Right then and there I knew how to solve the problem, or at least how to determine exactly where and what the problem was so it would be easy to solve. We simply needed proper tools!! We needed tools like the ones Felix had for testing circuits, only we did not have electronic circuits; we had a fluidic circuit.

Felix had a Volt-Ohm-Meter and an oscilloscope that he could attach at any point to his electronic circuit to determine exactly what the voltage was or what the electronic waveform looked like at that point. He had the tools to do this. Don and I had no such tools. We had a "circuit" of sorts: a fluidic circuit. We did not, however, have the equivalent of a Volt-Ohm-Meter or oscilloscope to attach at any point along the ten feet or so of tubing through which liquid flowed. Having such a tool would enable us to determine exactly where the problem was occurring.

I immediately told Don, and I suggested an approach for constructing a first tool, admittedly a very crude one. Don then consulted with another engineer, an optics expert, about how to construct it. We soon had a schematic diagram of a "snap on" optical measurement device with its own light emitting diode (LED) light source and photodetector that could be connected to the fluidic circuit at any point along its length. The optical measurement device could be connected to a chart recorder to follow the progress of samples flowing through the tubing versus time. This could be done at any point along the entire "circuit". The tool was analogous to an oscilloscope probe, which could be connected at any point along an electronic circuit to examine the waveform. Felix was delighted to build the first tool that the company had ever had to diagnose problems in fluidic circuits.

Felix built the tool, and Don and I tested it. We snapped it on at the beginning of the fluidic circuit and observed that the problematic sample type maintained its integrity and did not contaminate others early on. As we advanced our tool down the fluidic circuit path by clipping it onto the tubing at different points, we checked sample integrity going forward. It took only minutes to discover exactly where in the fluidic circuit the problem existed, as we traced the problematic sample all the way from the entrance and along its entire journey towards the instrument's optical analysis system at the far end of the tubing. We were able to pinpoint the exact spot where the problem originated, and just as Don had suggested, it turned out that the problem was caused by a particular fitting that allowed air to exit prior to readout of the sample. This time, however, we had unequivocal proof. This fitting was causing excessive spreading, especially of concentrated samples, and it was especially problematic for certain types of samples.

We not only found the problem quickly, but we were able to analyze its cause and design a new fitting that would avoid sample mixing. After fabricating and testing the new fitting, the problem was eliminated. With this problem solved, my boss was pleased, and my boss's boss was especially elated. The system moved into Manufacturing, orders were then being filled, and product was shipped out to customers. A week later, the Vice President of Product Engineering asked me to give a talk. He assembled an audience of about 50 people from Product Engineering. About 10 people from my department also attended, including my boss and boss's boss.

After my talk, the new tool for testing fluidic systems became part of the routine testing equipment used by both departments. Many such devices were fabricated by the company for use in testing and troubleshooting product prototypes. It was decided not to patent the technology but to keep it as a company trade secret, although a more advanced version was patented later on. I thus earned a reputation as someone who could come up with new ways to solve problems with fluidic systems. I didn't call it this then, but my thought process was exactly the same as what I've been describing to you in this book – namely, Dragonfly Thinking. What I did was to think from a high altitude, like a dragonfly. Flying high, I saw that Felix had tools and Don and I didn't. I then knew where to look to find an exact solution, even though I didn't have the specific expertise necessary to build the tool myself. But that was okay; help was available once the problem was pinpointed and understood. The key was the simple analogy between fluid circuits and electronic circuits that led to the realization that we did not have any testing tools, and that we could solve the problem we were working on much more quickly if the right tool could be developed.

Trouble with Feedback: The solution

Joe has invited Marty to a meeting with himself and Mitchell, the VP of Manufacturing:

Joe: "Mitchell, thanks for meeting with us. I believe my e-mail summarized our issue. I have some numbers to work with, but I also know that things have changed a bit this year. Jack is interested in the cost of extending the warranty period on our major products and also, in addition to the cost, the implications on your operations, especially Product Support, if we do this."

Mitchell: "I've asked a few key people to provide input, but I haven't heard back yet. Hopefully, I'll hear back by later today, but certainly by tomorrow – I'll send it along as soon as I get it. Also, if this goes into effect, we'll need to know what changes in procedures might be required and how this would impact our interface with Sales. Could you help with that?"

Joe: "Sure. Once we project the extended warranty expense, and if the program gets a green light, I can help work that out.

I also got this e-mail from Maria asking if there's anything in Manufacturing or Service, such as paperwork, which will show the end users how good we are at making and servicing our products? I have no idea what she may be thinking of or where she is going with this."

Mitchell: "Hmmmm..." (Picks up the phone) "Zaid, can you come in for a minute?" (To Joe and Marty) "Zaid is our Director of Quality Assurance."

Zaid enters Mitchell's office.

Mitchell: "Zaid, do you have one of the new Interdepartmental Quality Assurance (IQA) forms lying around? I'd like to show it to everyone at this meeting."

Zaid: "Sure, just a moment." (Zaid sends a text message. Two minutes later, an assistant enters with a handful of copies of the IQA form, and Zaid hands them out.)

Zaid: "This is a form we just recently put together for other departments. It hasn't gone out yet."

Marty: "Do you think this is the sort of thing Maria is looking for?"

Mitchell: "Knowing Maria, it could be."

Joe: "We'll find out."

Trouble with Feedback: Epilogue and Lessons

As it turned out, Maria loved the IQA form. She had it simplified for marketing purposes, and directed more to the end users so they could identify the exact product they purchased. This form was intended to show the end users that the company cared and wanted perfection, and the form did just that. The end users who purchased the products really connected with the company via that form, and were glad to send in feedback to get their extended warrantee. It was a perfect solution to a Big Important Problem.

This is, of course, a fictional story, but there are many lessons embedded in Marty's journey.

Marty first went about the task of refining and understanding his BIP, by speaking to a number of specialists in different areas. Each gave a different piece of the puzzle. This networking process led Marty to meeting a potential SMC, Jack. Marty understood the potential of this higher-up executive. He prepared diligently for his first meeting, and made sure that he made a strong first impression. It paid off with an SMC relationship. Next, Marty brainstormed many solutions with Briana and others, and came to a working solution. He effectively navigated the landscape of his business to get the job done, which is a critical factor in getting results. This is a key to effectively applying Dragonfly Thinking to any non-trivial problems.

"There is nothing more powerful than an idea whose time has come."

— VICTOR HUGO, AUTHOR OF *LES MISERABLES*, *THE HUNCHBACK OF NOTRE DAME*, AND OTHER GREAT NOVELS

Part 5:

Group Dragonfly Thinking – getting a team involved

20

Problem solving with groups or teams

Group problem solving uses the same approach (and flow diagram) as in Chapter 17: Solo Problem Solving: 8 Steps. You may recall that if you are relaxed and engaged you will increase your probability of generating, spotting, and recognizing good ideas. You can discipline yourself to stay engaged and even to relax on your own, but how do you do this in a group? If you don't use a correct strategy here, the group process will fail. You will have wasted everyone's time, and will have done less towards the problem solving effort than if you worked alone. You might even brew up confusion or apathy towards the problem, which could be counter-productive.

By learning how to properly guide a group process, you will be surprised with the results you can achieve. A group of minds can generate a lot of ideas and can combine them and take them to new levels. Different perspectives can help form entirely new solutions that no one person would have thought of alone. This process is usually called *brainstorming*. You must be careful here, though, since there are many approaches to brainstorming, and some may not work as well as others. The approach I will discuss in this chapter may be called *guided brainstorming using Dragonfly Thinking*. I have used it many times over, and it has consistently worked well for me.

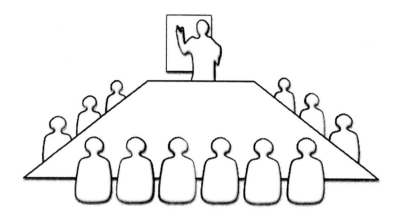

Some Basic Steps in Setting up a Group or Team Process

The most critical step in a group problem-solving process is to create an environment in which the participants feel uninhibited and completely free to produce ideas. Encourage team members to seek new and unique vantage points, and to continue to see things from a fresh perspective. If done properly, this will form a sort of chain reaction. An idea by one person will trigger three other people to produce new ideas, and so on. Again, ***at this stage, emphasize Quantity of ideas, not Quality***. There should be no criticism allowed. Encourage group members to state their ideas succinctly. Every individual group member should be encouraged to either add to an idea or to come up with a completely new one. Everything should be written down on a flip chart, and all finished sheets are then hung on the wall in full view of everyone. This brings us to our next general principle:

GENERAL PRINCIPLE E: Ideas are the fuel that make the impossible possible.

The more ideas you can generate, the better the chance of coming up with a novel solution to a difficult problem. But in order to have a free flow of ideas, it is first necessary not to judge, critique, limit, or otherwise influence your ideas or the idea generation process. This is true for an individual as well as for a group of individuals generating ideas. New vantage points and observations will lead to new solutions, and even unlikely ideas can contribute to this. New ideas will generate solutions that will become apparent, or may just pop out.

Although a formal group process in problem solving using Dragonfly Thinking is quite similar to the process used in solo problem solving in Chapter 17, the group or team must be set up properly and the right people recruited.

"The best way to have a good idea is to have lots of ideas."
— LINUS PAULING, ONE OF THE FEW RECIPIENTS OF TWO NOBEL PRIZES

Time Constraints and Complexity

What if you are time constrained? What if you need a solution to a problem yesterday? Or what if a problem is so hopelessly complicated, you can't imagine tackling it all by yourself. Any of these conditions may be enough to raise your blood pressure to boiling, but group problem solving may help. When you leverage multiple minds on a problem, you can often exponentially increase your capabilities, as the diverse backgrounds of group members can greatly expand the breadth of possible ideas. Before we get into the mechanics of it, let's have a case study showing the kind of problem that calls for a group process, and the general structure of the solution process:

21
The Marketing Smiley

The situation that follows is fictitious but could easily happen. You can try to solve this problem with a small group, and see how your results compare with the results developed here.

This case study also displays a very typical and important element of BIPs: that often, they involve issues that others have overlooked because they seem not worth effort to delve into. By taking a seemingly trivial problem very seriously, you may be able to come up with new solutions that are far more innovative than any others. Don't underestimate the importance of any part of a BIP!

Problem: Can you draw this smiley face without making any extra lines and without even once lifting the pencil off of the paper after it makes initial contact?

You work for the brand development department of the high profile public relations and marketing firm: BrandXBrandY, Inc. Your department has been thrust into the center of an intense effort to obtain a lucrative contract worth many millions of dollars. You are competing with another firm for this big client contract. Your firm and the competing firm are the only players left after all other competing companies were eliminated from a larger field of competitors by the Client. The Client decided that either of the two remaining firms could do this important work, and everyone has been at a standstill, waiting for the Client to make a decision.

The Client has now issued an e-mail to the Executive VP of your firm, who is the contact person. In the email, the client indicates its decision to pick the more creative of the two firms, since, after the contract is signed, a series of creative marketing campaigns will be essential for success. To pick the firm to go forward with, the Client has decided to set up a little contest. The contest involves solving the smiley face puzzle. The smiley face, which forms part of the Client's logo, must be drawn in the contest according to a simple rule, as quoted from the Client's e-mail:

"The following face ☺ must be drawn without making any extra lines and without even once lifting the pencil off of the paper after it makes initial contact." The Client has made this even more difficult by adding the following additional conditions: "This will have to be demonstrated three (3) times, and you can elect to supply the paper. Each firm will send a representative in exactly one week to our main office to perform this exercise. Representatives will be asked to perform independently in separate rooms. The winner of the contest and of the contract will be the firm whose representative performs best."

You have been put in charge of coming up with the approach to be used by your firm's representative. What do you do?

How can you secure this lucrative contract for your firm? You can give it your best shot, but what is your best shot?

It is now Friday afternoon. You know that you have exactly one week until the contest will be held. You call a meeting for Monday morning. After the weekend, the team members will have a fresh start to look at this problem. On Monday morning you assemble your problem solving team, consisting of twelve talented people. Counting today, there are four full days left before Friday, the day of the contest. In the conference room, you post the assignment in large print on the wall so that all can read it. You make sure to have an easel with a flip chart so that one of the team members can write down all ideas generated by your team.

Probing the landscape

You first generate a series of possible solutions by asking the team to brainstorm freely. You ask the team to fly, to soar high above the problem and look down upon it. You ask the following question: "If you step back from the problem and try to decipher its landscape, what features do you see?" "Fly over it and describe the terrain." You are essentially asking the team to reformulate the problem.

The team comes up with the following statements:

1. How can we draw a smiley face without making any extra lines, and without even once lifting the pencil off of the paper after it makes initial contact?

2. How can we determine the significance of the drawing having to be done three times?

3. How can we capitalize on the requirement that we can elect to supply the paper, and should we elect to do so?

4. How can we determine the qualifications for our representative who will do the actual drawing?

5. How can we determine whether there is significance to the representatives of the opposing companies being situated in separate rooms?

6. How can our representative perform best so we become the winner of the contest and of the contract?

Each statement may be viewed as an aerial view of a portion of terrain of the stated problem, as seen by a dragonfly. In order to explore the details of the problem further, you decide to break the team into two groups, with each group handling 3 of the six areas of the problem terrain. Group A handles the odd numbered areas while Group B handles the even ones. Each group generates ideas: as many as possible.

Mapping Terrain

In this exercise with Groups A and B, it is important to seek quantity of ideas, not quality. Any idea is accepted, no matter how ridiculous it may seem. Everything gets written down on a flip chart. If the exercise is done by two groups, then there are two flip charts. One group is led by you, the discussion leader, and the other group is headed by the domain expert – e.g. a problem solving whiz – that you have selected for this task. There is no discussion, and especially no criticism allowed: only ideas.

You encourage each group to think through each assigned area of problem terrain in different ways. You also encourage members of each group to add additional ideas to the ideas already generated, as long as the exercise doesn't become repetitious. For example, in terrain area number 3: since your firm can supply the paper, how can this be used to advantage?

Some of the ideas generated are:

- ☐ We use paper that is easy to erase, in case our representative makes a mistake.
- ☐ We use paper with the eyes and mouth already on it, and just draw the circle.
- ☐ We use paper with the smiley face already on it: problem solved!

In the next step, each group presents its ideas to the entire team for terrain areas 1 through 6. In each case, flip chart paper sheets with the ideas are fastened to the wall with masking tape, so all can see them. Soon, the wall is covered with all of the generated ideas on the 6 terrain areas. This is the dragonfly view of the problem expanded into possible interpretations.

Merging landmarks

Next, you consider the overall problem in context of these terrain area interpretations. Again, you use a flip chart. You, as the discussion leader, maintain an orderly and sequential discussion of the entire problem, with ideas being generated now towards a solution. As before, everything gets written down. There is no discussion, and especially no criticism allowed: only ideas. You encourage your team to think through the areas of problem terrain in different ways. You also encourage them to add additional ideas to the ideas already generated, creating new hybrid ideas. After the team has exhausted their creativity for the time being, you break for coffee, cookies, and fruit.

Upon reconvening, all of the flip charts with the ideas are now on the wall in a separate area from the other chart paper. You now ask the team to group ideas that are similar. You then ask the team to go over the list of groups by voting. Voting is done through secret ballot, by each team member dropping a vote into the appropriate box, or by placing votes in the form of adhesive-backed symbols directly onto the flip chart page (multivoting, e.g. with dots). By doing this, you are now able to obtain a consensus to identify the groups of ideas that could possibly work and that would be acceptable to the client. You break for lunch. Idea groups with the fewest votes are eliminated and the others carried forward. The voting process can be repeated, if necessary.

In the afternoon, the team organizes the remaining groups of ideas and numbers the ideas that have survived and appear workable. Finally, you have a list of 12 ideas that could possibly work. They are listed as follows:

Final Ideas

The groups of ideas that were selected by vote follow. When the ideas were first moved from their original position into a group, each group was given a name. Then the vote was taken. The groups with the greatest number of votes remain. The last step was to number the remaining ideas, in order.

I. Technique Solutions (Solutions relying on special techniques)

1. Draw the circle. Roll the pencil on its side, making sure to always have part of the pencil in contact with the paper, especially when lifting the pencil tip off the paper. Then roll the pencil into position where one eye should be made. Carefully lift the pencil to its original tip-down position and draw the first eye. Roll the pencil down again, and repeat this process for the other eye and the mouth.

2. Use a very thin sheet of flexible paper. First draw the circle. Holding the pencil steady, move the portion of the paper up

against the pencil point where one eye should be drawn, and draw the first eye without lifting the point. Repeat for the other eye and for the mouth. Keep the pencil point engaged with the paper at all times.

3. Tape a corner of the paper to the pencil with some adhesive tape. Be sure that the paper is taped so that it is always in contact with the pencil. Then draw the face, making sure the tape does not fall off, and the corner of the paper sheet is always engaged with the pencil as you lift the point to draw the features of the smiley face. Although you are lifting the pencil point, with this method the pencil is never lifted off of the paper, since it is always touching the paper.

4. Grab a corner of the paper. Hold it firmly against the pencil about 2 or 3 inches from the pencil point while you draw the face on the paper with the point. The drawing technique is similar here to that used in solution No. 3, except that there is no need for tape.

- - - - - -   - - - - - -   - - - - - -   - - - - - -   - - - -
- -   - - - - - -

II. Gimmicks (Solutions relying on special apparatus)

5. Use a mechanical pencil. Start by drawing a circle. Then slowly withdraw the lead, keeping the mechanical pencil pressed to the paper. Slide the pencil tip to the position for the first eye. Push out the pencil lead again to draw the eye; then retract the lead. Repeat the process until the second eye and mouth have been drawn.

6. Place the pencil on the surface of a blank sheet of paper on the table and, meanwhile, draw the smiley face with your pen. It doesn't matter if you lift the pen to draw the eyes and mouth.

The pencil still never leaves the paper.

7. Use a flexible rubber pencil, obtainable from a magician's supply store. While holding the eraser firmly down against the paper, bend the writing tip of the pencil down to the paper and draw the smiley face. You can start with a circle, and it doesn't matter if you lift the writing tip from the paper while drawing the eyes and mouth, since pressing down on the eraser ensures that the pencil is in contact with the paper at all times.

- - - - - -   - - - - - -   - - - - - -   - - - - - -   - - - -

- -   - - - - - -

III. Pre-Drawing and/or Pre-Printed Paper

8. Start with a piece of paper where the eyes and mouth are already printed. Draw a circle around the eyes and mouth with the pencil, and you are finished.

9. Start with a piece of paper with an opening parenthesis character and a colon as, shown between the two square brackets [(:]. Draw a circle around the parenthesis character and colon, keeping the pencil on the paper, and then turn the paper 90 degrees counter clockwise so you can see the smiley face.

10. Start with the same paper as in No. 6, but use a colon followed by a closing parenthesis character, as such: [:)]. Draw a circle around the parenthesis character and colon, keeping the pencil on the paper, and then turn the paper 90 degrees clockwise so you can see the smiley face.

- - - - - -   - - - - - -   - - - - - -   - - - - -

- - - - - -   - - - - - -

IV. Pre-Printed Paper and Different Meaning of Key Word

11. Print the smiley face on the paper in advance. When starting the drawing, lay the paper on the table or desk with the smiley face on the upper side in full view. Now place the pencil on the paper. Pulling from the edge, draw the paper toward you. Thus you have "drawn" the smiley face, and the pencil has never left the paper. (This solution uses different interpretation of the word *drawn*.).

12. Start with the smiley face already on the paper. Place the pencil eraser on the surface of the paper. Press down on the pencil, applying firm pressure to the eraser to create friction against the sheet of paper. Using the eraser, draw the paper toward you across the table. Thus, you have drawn the smiley face, as well.

The four groups of ideas can be used to remap the terrain, with each group forming a terrain sector. A fifth terrain sector may be added, should any new ideas be developed at this stage that fall outside of the four sectors.

- - - - - -   - - - - - -   - - - - - -   - - - - - -   - - - -
- -   - - - - - -

Wow! 12 viable solutions were developed by your team during the problem solving session. The team did a great job. It wasn't so obvious at first that this many solutions could be generated. If you try, you can probably generate even more solutions. Things might look quite promising right now, but which solution is best? There are still three days left until the day of the contest.

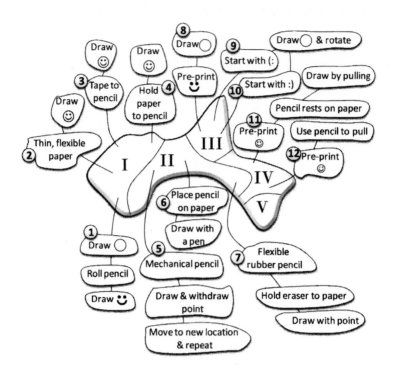

DRAGONFLY TERRAIN DIAGRAM

The Contest has Changed

The following morning a new e-mail comes in from the Client. It says: "We will supply the pencil."

Now things may be a bit more complicated. You immediately assemble the team. A new set of ideas emerges when you ask for pitfalls. What if the Client chooses to supply a pencil that has no eraser? What if it is a brand new pencil with no point? Either of these would tend to eliminate certain solutions. Nos. 1 and 2 would not work if the pencil has no point, nor would Nos. 3 or 4. No 6 still seem workable, but what about Nos. 5 and 7? Would solution No. 5 still work? The representative could bring his or her own mechanical pencil and place the supplied pencil on the paper the whole time. But what if the client considers a mechanical pencil to be a pencil that they didn't supply? No. 7 is now questionable also, since the Client may consider a rubber pencil as a "pencil" that they did not supply. No. 12 depends upon having an eraser, and that solution would not work if the sly client supplies a pencil without an eraser and if, for example, the pencil is sharpened with a writing point at each end. No. 8 would not work if the pencil supplied by the Client is unsharpened, and no pencil sharpener is available. Could the representative bring a pencil sharpener along, just in case? The same logic applies to Nos. 9 and 10. No. 11 should still work.

The team comes up with the best remaining solutions: Nos. 6 and 11. The team also decides that Nos. 8, 9, and 10 should also still work if the representative brings a pencil sharpener or modifies these solutions by bringing a pen and placing the supplied pencil flat on the paper. These solutions are additionally good because they all appear to have a high chance of working three times in a row, as specified by the rules. If a pencil sharpener is brought along, Nos. 1, 2, 3, and 4 may also work. What if No. 12 were modified to allow the pencil to be placed flat upon the paper and pressed down to pull (draw) the paper along the table? In that way the solution would not be dependent upon an eraser. No. 12 was considered a bit risky by the team, since without the eraser the pencil might slip. The selection of a final solution has not yet been achieved, and it is agreed to adjourn until the next day.

Turmoil

Another e-mail from the Client arrives the following morning: **"Also, we may choose to blindfold the representatives prior to the contest."**

Now, with your team having figured out how best to solve the smiley face puzzle, your representative must also be prepared to perform this task blindfolded. How weird is that!

You bring the team together again. There are only two days left until the big day of the contest. How can this latest barrier be overcome? The team examines the solutions again and decides that Nos. 1 – 4 could not be performed blindfolded with a high degree of confidence. Group I is out. No. 6, the remaining best solution from Group II, is still possible, even blindfolded. But the remaining solutions from Groups III and IV now look more attractive. One of the group members points out that Group IV solutions could be modified so that the supplied paper has a rough side and a smooth side, or some similar tactile cue, to let a blindfolded representative know on which side of the paper the smiley face had been printed. No. 11 from Group IV is now voted to be the most attractive solution, with No. 12 in second place, followed by No. 6 as a distant third.

The contest

The following day, with one day left before the contest, everyone is anxious to see if another communication will come from the Client. There is none. Finally, on the day of the contest, your firm goes forward with Solution No. 11: a pre-printed smiley face with a pencil resting on the paper. The representative succeeds in the challenge easily, and your company wins the contract, because the solution was creative and easy to demonstrate three times. A happy ending!

22
General guidelines for meetings

As seen in the previous case study, a well-guided brainstorming meeting can provide superb solutions to problems. However, it is also important to recognize that poorly run meetings can be a big waste of time. This is true of any meeting, and includes brainstorming sessions. The key to an effective brainstorming session is to foster a free flow of ideas that address the problem from different and perhaps unique vantage points, as I will highlight below.

Brainstorming sessions can be greatly amplified in larger groups, but with larger groups *group management* also becomes much more important – i.e., keeping everyone engaged and involved. This is typically the responsibility of the Discussion Leader, Chair, or Moderator. A well-run brainstorming session can surprise all of the participants, and most importantly, can lead to solutions.

Every meeting should have a purpose, and most should have an agenda. If at all possible, you should provide these to participants in advance. This may be as simple as telling everyone the problem you will be tackling.

As with nearly all meetings, it is important to adhere strictly to the set amount of time for a brainstorming session. In general, it's better to set more time than you'll need than less – you can always end early. Estimating the time it takes to solve a problem is very difficult, but this will become easier with experience. It is also perfectly acceptable to end with a set of possible solutions and continue the meeting at another time, particularly if you know that the same team can be reassembled a day or two later. In fact, splitting a meeting into multiple sessions can be helpful, as it can activate the Iceberg Principle (see Chapter 16).

Planning for a productive meeting

A well-guided group brainstorming session should feel similar to a brainstorming session between just a few individuals. There are a few simple guidelines for ensuring that this happens, and for making a session a success.

The guidelines for an effective guided brainstorming session are a bit more specific than those for a typical meeting. Guidelines for a typical meeting are:

- Clarify the purpose of the meeting beforehand, and also at the start.
- Make an agenda available beforehand, and actually follow it in the meeting.
- Invite the right people.
- Don't go over the allotted time.
- Develop action items by the end of the meeting.
- Assign specific actions and determine next steps.

For a guided brainstorming session, all of these elements apply, but you also must be very intentional in creating the right kind of atmosphere. Every member should feel free to contribute ideas, even if they are not totally feasible, without fear of being shut down.

Suggested steps in a guided brainstorming meeting to ensure and maintain the right atmosphere are:

1. Relaxation.
2. Introductions.
3. Refreshments.
4. Ideas from everyone.
5. Breaks.
6. Option to shut down and reconvene later.
7. Remembering to thank everyone for what *"we"* did.

GENERAL PRINCIPLE F: For group problem solving, start recruiting the first team member first.

It is much easier to assemble a problem solving team if you've already convinced one person of the importance of the problem you're facing. With this first person on board, forming a team becomes much easier. This is especially true if he can co-lead the effort.

TACTICAL PROCESS 5: Running effective group brainstorming meetings

There are two phases to effective group brainstorming sessions: preparation and execution. Each requires some care to get it right. The preparation mostly involves assembling your team and setting the ground rules. Here are a few key points to keep in mind when planning a group brainstorming session:

1. Ideally, you'll want to invite between 6 and 12 people to your brainstorming session. More than that is usually unhelpful.

2. Decide on a Discussion Leader, and be sure he or she is up to speed on the important points to discuss.

3. Be prepared to establish ground rules at the start of the meeting, and make sure the Discussion Leader understands and is ready to enforce them.

Once you've started your meeting, some good guidelines are as follows:

- *Seek quantity, not quality, of ideas.*
- Follow the problem solving steps laid out in Tactical Process 4:
    1. Survey the problem from different vantage points, like the dragonfly.
    2. Encourage group members to use their domain experience to help stimulate ideas.
    3. Break up the problem into sub problems; redefine it to generate more ideas.
    4. Recombine, link, or add ideas.
    5. Take a short break if needed.
    6. Consolidate ideas into groups that can be named.
    7. Rank the groups to select the best one, and repeat the process, if necessary.
    8. Select the group most likely to succeed, and work towards a compelling solution.
- During the process, write down and display all ideas.
- When the best solution is defined or the meeting concludes, plan action items.

Note that this process is very similar to that outlined in the 8-steps for problem solving (Tactical Process 4), but involves a few differences that make it more suited for groups. Also, it is important to remember that the most critical element is to **create an environment that encourages, and never stifles, creativity** – even if some suggested ideas are implausible or impossible.

Size of Team or Group

As indicated in steps above, an effective brainstorming team consists typically of six to twelve individuals, but could include more or less depending upon the mix of people. Generally, between six and twelve is optimal, and larger groups should be split up to solve sub-problems.

Dissolution into Subgroups

Although the group can be divided, a critical mass of at least 5 or six people is necessary for group process to emerge and be truly effective. I've been involved in complex problem solving sessions with at least a dozen groups of about 10 to 12 people in each group, all meeting at the same time. You can imagine the complexity involved, not to mention the cost of everyone's time and effort. Meetings, in general, are costly. In solving Big problems, however, extra time spent on solutions can be paid back many times over. Dividing effort in order to run things in parallel is cost effective, provided that the process is well run.

Effective Team Performance: General Approaches

The Discussion Leader, Chair, or Moderator sets the tone for a meeting. I've found it useful to post the ground rules for team brainstorming sessions in large font, so everyone can see them at all times. When someone violates a rule, or is not taking advantage of a rule, the Discussion Leader merely points to the written rule that has been violated or that might be of help in the particular situation. The team leader need not make an issue out of it: merely pointing is often enough.

Typical Posted Rules to Facilitate Dragonfly Thinking

1. State an idea in 30 seconds or less.
2. Absolutely no criticism of any kind allowed.
3. Quantity and breadth of ideas is key, not quality (yet).
4. Modify existing ideas or add to them.
5. Use the ideas of others as launch pads to arrive at new vantage points and come up with totally new ideas.

Voting

When you must determine which ideas or groups of ideas are best, it is time to vote. I've found this to be effective, as it enables everyone to share in the outcome. You can use a closed ballot, or, in my preferred method, you can give each team member some stickers or other markers to attach to their option of choice on a flip chart. Participants can place multiple markers, allowing them to grade multiple options based on their perceived quality.

Brain warm-up exercises

I was a relatively new employee working for a large hospital supply company. My job was business development – identifying new products for distribution and new companies for possible joint ventures or acquisition. We had an annual meeting with the Big Boss (that is, my boss's, boss's boss), who headed the largest division of the company, and everyone was nervous as this meeting day grew closer. One day, during a relaxed moment, I shared a brain teaser with my boss. He became very animated. "The Big Boss likes things like that," he said, "you should give it to him." On the day of the meeting I tried it, and it was a major success. Not only did the Big Boss like the brain teaser, but it created a positive tone for the whole meeting.

The experience in giving a brain teaser to the right person, in the case above to the Big Boss, taught me a valuable lesson. A brain teaser given in the right context is a game, and putting people into a playful mode is key to both creativity and to generating comfort, with individuals or in groups. An animated debate for a few minutes over a funny or clever brainteaser can be a great way to warm people up, to get them thinking in ways they usually repress in rote work functions. A good brainteaser should get people thinking like kids, thinking outside of ordinary boundaries, and will put the meeting in a strong frame that it is okay to be playful in tackling the Big problem. I have done this many times, and it has been profoundly effective.

I recommend giving a simple brain teaser to a problem solving team at the very beginning of a brainstorming session. About 5 minutes on it is all that is really needed. This may even allow time for a few brain teasers, but the focus should always be on the creative frame that you're setting. Once you feel that the energy is right, move into work on the actual problem. I've also played with brainteasers when I'm problem solving alone, and they can be great thought stimulators or ways of getting out of a rut.

You will find several brain teasers that follow. These are simple, and some are relatively easy. There are additional brain teasers in Appendix 2, some of which are more difficult than the brain teasers in this chapter. Again, the most important thing is to get people thinking differently, so find whatever brainteasers or games that will do it for you.

The brain teasers that follow have been selected as possible warm-up exercises for group problem solving sessions. The answers follow at the end of Part 5.

1. A bookkeeper noted a balloon floating outside his window while he was doing some financial work and quickly realized that the word balloon has two double letters in a row: two o's and two l's. He then wondered to himself: "Is there a word with three double letters in a row?" Can you think of one?

2. "Twist of fiction": was a crossword puzzle question. Can you think of the six letter word in response? (This one can be quite difficult if you don't see it right away.)

3. Can you find the two missing letters in the sequence below? (This falls into the same category as the previous one: if you don't see it early on it may take a long time before you do.) O T T _ F _ S E N T

4. What word is used before "speed" and after "time"? (Hint: it has four letters.)

5. What goes all around the world but stays in the corner?

6. What is the beginning of eternity, the end of time and space, the beginning of every end, and the end of every place?

7. What has 18 legs and catches flies?

8. Flat on the ground, yet 100 feet up in the air. What is it?

23

Forming a stellar problem solving team

The team that you collect for your problem solving can be the key to powerful solutions. Building a good team requires intuition and experience, but there are general guidelines:

First off, you should not set out to form a group first and then select problems. Although some organizations do this, a problem solving team is most effective if it is specific. Solving a big problem is like a journey, and the team must be as organic as the journey's challenges. In the course of solving a BIP, you'll notice an evolution, in that some team members will join up and others will drift out as it becomes clear that their expertise isn't totally relevant to the problem. This is normal and natural, and shouldn't cause any distress. Over time, your group's strengths will calibrate to the problem. Sometimes even you, who are the key person who started it all, will need to take a back seat and let others drive the bus down the road.

Different Roles encountered on Teams

If you are the initiator of a problem solving quest, and if you wish to advance your career by selecting an important problem and assembling a team, what should your role in the problem solving process be? How can you retain credit for your work and later have a lion's share in the glory of success? There are three possibilities here:

1. You can be the Discussion Leader or Chair.
2. You can be the Team Expert.
3. You can be the Organizer (and just sit back).

You should seek a variety of perspectives and skills for your problem solving team. It is important to know how to identify, and to appreciate, different types of team players, and the various strengths that each can provide. This next section describes a number of different personality types or team roles. Note, these roles are not mutually exclusive, and often several roles will overlap in the same person. Finding members to serve all of these roles can help with a good team dynamic.

Discussion Leader, Chair, or Moderator

The Discussion Leader is the chairperson of the meeting, and orchestrates the discussion by focusing the powerful team resources on the problem to be solved. Often, but not always, the best person to choose as Discussion Leader is a highly organized and logical thinker. Some Discussion Leaders will ask all participants to write down their ideas at the start of the meeting. Others will obtain ideas verbally from participants and write them down as they're shared with the group. The Discussion Leader must work harmoniously with Team Experts to run the team meeting, and should have a feel for the styles of the various participants.

There may be multiple experts on a given team. It is important that the Discussion Leader not allow any one expert to dominate the discussion and sway others to his or her point of view. The most important consideration is to allow the ideas from even the most renowned expert to flow in with other ideas, and to be loosening, rather than inhibiting, to the creativity of others. All views must be given equal weight until the brainstorming session has ended.

There may also be one (or more than one) extremely introverted person(s) on the team. Introverts generally prefer to share their views with one person, not a whole group of people. However, their views are often important and sometimes pivotal. They must not be lost, as would be the case if a person is quiet and does not contribute to the discussion. It is the Discussion Leader's job to make sure that every person is comfortable in expressing views and that everyone's views are heard by all members of the team.

One approach is for the discussion leader to make eye contact with the introverted individual and to ask: "Are there any other ideas?" Another approach is to ask: "Could we hear from some of the quieter people in the room now?" All of this is a matter of style and circumstance, and will depend on the particular people and the team. The Discussion Leader can also, at appropriate times, invite the participants to step outside of their ordinary perspectives and to take different views of the problem. This way, they can explore entirely new and perhaps non-obvious solutions.

Team Expert or Facilitator

A Team Expert is a person with extensive domain knowledge relevant to the specific problem. Typically, at the start of a problem solving session, the Team Expert will state the problem and provide some further insight and perhaps detail associated with the problem. Also, the expert can step in here and there and help guide towards new, non-obvious areas that might not yet be obvious.

I will sometimes assign a Team Expert the role of scribe, i.e., the one who lists all solutions or steps provided by the team members on a flip chart. His superior grasp of the problem's specific details may allow him to clarify or crystallize (but not to significantly alter!!) ideas from other members as he puts them on the board. I prefer a Team Expert versus the discussion leader as the scribe, since you want the scribe committed to capturing all the ideas.

Organizer

If you are the person who started the problem solving quest but are not comfortable as a Discussion Leader or as a Team Expert, or alternatively if you have decided that there are people on the team better suited for those jobs, you can still participate as the Organizer. At team meetings, you can mainly sit back and watch, as well as contribute ideas. In the Organizer role, you will schedule the meetings, keep everyone in the loop as things happen, and take good notes. You may also from time to time exchange thoughts informally with any senior or experienced people who have attended team meetings or who are keeping an eye on the team's progress. Any important insights that are extracted from these conversations should be shared with appropriate team members, such as the Discussion Leader and the Team Expert or Facilitator. The Organizer's role becomes primary in-between meetings, when attention and momentum towards solutions must be upheld.

Team Players

One or more Team Players are highly desirable. Team players are optimistic people with good social intuition, and a natural ability to keep people motivated and engaged. You probably know some of these types of people – they are able to disarm tension in social situations, and they naturally exude relaxation and ease to the people around them. They are fantastic in group problem solving, as they help maintain the spirit and cohesiveness of the group, especially when things aren't going well. I've often found good team players to be Senior or Experienced People.

Logical Thinkers

Logical thinkers are always a good addition to a problem solving team. They can arrive at a consequence given premises or background information using logic and experience. In addition, Logical Thinkers can explain to everyone on the team exactly how they arrive at a conclusion. I often find these types of people to be good choices for the group moderator or leader, as the logical thought process can help focus the whole meeting and keep things on track.

Experts and Resource People

Experts and resource people provide a wealth of domain knowledge, or in other words, they have deep and extensive knowledge or experience in the area thought to be most relevant to the problem at hand. Members of the problem solving group will often turn to these experts later on in the process, in order to get an assessment of a certain proposed solution.

Senior and Experienced People

Senior and Experienced People are those who know the organization and know how to get things done and implement solutions. They will often be able to orchestrate how you *should* or *should not* proceed with a particular approach in the organization. They can act as sponsors, or might have access to sponsors, to help implement action items.

Spatial Visual People

Spatial Visual People are the so called "right-brained people". Naturally, most people use both hemispheres of their brain – the right hemisphere being more associated with holistic interpretations, and the left being more associated with critical details. But some individuals favor the left hemisphere and they tend to be more fact- and time-oriented, while others favor the right hemisphere, and tend to be more concept- and big picture-oriented. In her milestone book: "Upside-Down Brilliance, The Visual Spatial Learner," Linda Kreger Silverman, PhD, describes extreme right-brained people as often the very best problem solvers, when put into the proper focus and context. In a group problem solving session, these individuals can be exceptionally powerful. Since they tend to approach the world through concepts (rather than through specific facts), they often develop their own methods of problem solving, and can generate unusual solutions to problems. In a group problem solving atmosphere, their perspectives can be critical.

Other team members

The team members listed are just a sampling of types of individuals that I've encountered on problem solving teams, and it portrays some of their characteristic contributions to the process. There may be many more types of people who can contribute to a successful solution. Your judgment should guide you in forming the most useful team for a given problem.

Solutions to brainteasers from Chapter 22

1. Bookkeeper
2. Oliver
3. **F** and **S** to fill in the missing words **Five** and **Six** in the series:

One Two Three Four Five Six Seven Eight Nine Ten

4. The word is "warp".
5. A postage stamp.
6. The letter "e".
7. A baseball team.
8. A dead millipede.

Part 6:
Problem solving and the future

24

Robotic problem solvers and you

Important news came on the evening of February 16, 2011, when Watson, an artificial intelligence machine created by IBM, defeated the world's best players at the game *Jeopardy*. Ken Jennings, famous for winning 74 games in a row on the TV quiz show Jeopardy, reportedly wrote on his video screen beneath his final answer of the game: "I, for one, welcome our new computer overlords."

(A Jeopardy question for the reader: *The popular cartoon that popularized the overlords quote.*)

Although Watson had flaws, it clearly emerged as a victor and the herald of a new generation of question answering artificial intelligence machines. Now, if a machine has instantaneous access to massive databases and can respond to nuances in human speech to find answers quickly, what will this mean for the many types of workers who currently spend considerable time looking things up or servicing customers?

This is not to mention what robotics will mean for workers who perform repetitive tasks, such as in manufacturing. Hon Hai Precision Industry Co., Ltd. (trading as Foxconn) a multinational electronics manufacturing company headquartered in Taiwan, is the world's largest maker of electronic components. This company assembles Apple products, employs 1 million workers in China, and signed a deal this past year to purchase 1 million robots over the next three years from the European company ABB. The robots will be performing repetitive work and will not replace workers, at least initially. It is likely that many workers will now be attending to the robots. However, when production volumes increase substantially, no new workers will be hired. This scenario is similar to that which transpired in the automobile manufacturing industry in the US. It is fairly certain that in the not so far future, machines will be doing a lot of the jobs that humans now do.

But despite all this, one of the very last areas that intelligent machines will conquer is the realm of complex problem solving. You can be sure that solving BIPs will remain a human endeavor for a long time. If you develop problem solving skills, you will not become obsolete. The reason for human dominance in the problem solving arena is that it requires information from many sources of different types, often including many people. It requires completely novel thinking and synthesis of loosely related data types, which has proven exceptionally difficult to program into a computer. And it requires the confidence and the willingness of others in order to understand the full intricacy of a BIP and to begin to explore possible solutions.

Albert Einstein said: "We can't solve problems by using the same kind of thinking we used when we created them."

The expertise required to solve a BIP may for a long time require human interaction, human-based fact finding, skepticism, idea generation, and follow-up. A good problem solver relies on his ability to radically change thinking modes depending upon the information, context, and emotional content of an obstacle. But even switching between distinct thought patterns is often not enough, because entirely *new* patterns might be required to gain a solution. This is the essence of Einstein's statement. The ability to look at a problem from a hundred feet up in the air, and then to examine the same problem close up, may be expected to remain a human activity for a long time to come.

25
What's next?

Robots

We have entered an era that will see a dramatic increase in the use of automation, computerized systems, and robots. Robots have actually been with us for some time, especially since the dawn of the US space program which led to the development of smaller semiconductors and the computer revolution. Robots have landed on Mars and have explored areas of Martian terrain for extended time periods. Robotic systems have been sent into deep space and are now passing the outer planets of the solar system.

Robotics continues to advance at an ever increasing rate. From robotic vacuum cleaners for the home to robotic surgical systems for the hospital, more and more robotic applications are finding their way into common use. Some robots in the near future will be human-like, and may even have near-human faces and the ability to perceive and even to display emotions. Early prototypes of some such robots have already been built.

Imagine in this new world that intelligent machines service your calls to a company such as an airline, a hotel, a utility, or even a restaurant. You may not only hear a voice on the telephone, but view a real-time image of the speaking face on your smartphone. In effect, this computerized system will become the *voice* and the *face* of the company or service provider that you are dealing with.

ROBOCAT

If this seems farfetched, recall that the iPhone 4S, released in October 2011, has a voice recognition operator called *Siri*, which is able to interpret and respond to the desires of a user. Siri, operating on a cellphone, is a pale shade of what is likely to come. Polite or snarky or perhaps even cuddly robotic systems – like speaking tabbies or cute canine robots – may dominate the marketing world of the near future. Other robots will undoubtedly greet you at the door like a butler and may seem almost human. Robots and robotic systems will take care of the elderly, which is already starting to happen in Japan. There are definite upsides to a robotized world! But robots will make problem solving, a uniquely human endeavor, ever more critical for the workers of the near future.

Cloud Computing and Decentralization

Data processing has become more decentralized with cloud computing. Businesses are also becoming more and more decentralized, and contracting as opposed to hiring permanent employees is on the increase and may be the way of the future, which makes problem solving with teams across various areas of expertise especially important, but also changes the types of challenges that will be faced.

Although the introduction of robotic systems and other new technologies will replace workers, and jobs will be lost, new problems will always crop up, and problem solvers will be needed. A robot (or any device) that relies too much on the cloud is at risk of becoming useless if disconnected. We're seeing this a bit in mobile devices now too. Of course talking on the phone and web browsing are necessarily connected actions, but certain other functions can benefit from an offline mode (particularly in the case of mapping where location can be determined from GPS satellites even without cell coverage).

There are security and authentication concerns too. Someone could spoof the cloud service and provide the robot with fake or malicious instructions. Inevitably the world will be slowly transformed by technology, and new opportunities as well as new problems will emerge.

Manufacturing

To reduce costs in manufacturing, many companies nowadays are turning to countries with cheap labor. Conversely, many industries are turning to automation via machines or robotics. When automation and robotic systems have been introduced into an industry, there is initially a strong need for supervisors to insure smooth operation and to assure quality. Long term, however, the automation will greatly reduce the number of jobs. Workers skilled in the old ways will be laid off. This is happening in many industries and is expected to happen globally at an increasing rate. Robots are being introduced especially into manufacturing industries where the work is dull, dirty, or dangerous (3 d's), but as the robots become smarter, they will be able to displace more and more complex jobs.

In the US, some predict that this trend will continue, and jobs will be lost unless we increase our manufacturing base. Others suggest that there will be an inevitable shift of manufacturing to countries with cheaper labor, and that to generate growth and wealth, the US must develop radically new, post-industrial approaches. With the huge capabilities provided by the internet and the general explosion of technology in the last decade, I am a firm believer in the latter. We must become a nation of problem solvers.

Innovation

Alvin Toffler, author or coauthor of "Future Shock," "The Third Wave," "Power Shift," and "Revolutionary Wealth," refers to Daniel Bell, who established the idea of the *post-industrial society* in his 1973 work "The Coming of Post-Industrial Society." In this seminal work, Bell correctly predicted many attributes of today's economy, such as the global diffusion of capital, the imbalance of international trade, and the decline of the manufacturing sector on the U.S. domestic front. Toffler and others say we must innovate. Innovation results in new technologies and new business models.

Innovation is usually born out of tackling BIPs and solving them. Business innovation and technology development will likely be drivers of economic growth in technologically advanced countries like the US.

As a model for today's economic shifts, Toffler cites the agricultural revolution, which once dominated the US but later gave way to the industrial revolution. He proposes that the industrial age is now giving way to something else. New systems and models became necessary with each of these major shifts and will also be needed in this new economy. Toffler also cites public and private education through high school as being badly in need of revamping for the economy of the future.

Although robotic systems and other new technologies will replace future workers, and fewer new jobs will be created along these fronts, different jobs, and many new types of problems, will continually arise. And guess what? Problem solvers will be needed.

Mobile Workforce

Daniel H. Pink, in his book "Free Agent Nation" (published in 2001) describes a country whose labor force is increasingly composed of *free agents*. By *free agents* Pink refers to solo professionals, freelancers, independent contractors, consultants, and other self-employed workers – basically, anyone whose work lies outside of the traditional organization-job structure of the industrial age. According to Pink, in 2001 there were already 33 million free agents or "disorganization" men and women in the US, more than a quarter of the entire American workforce. Today this number is much greater. These individuals do not show up in unemployment data or labor statistics. Most individuals in this sector arrived not by choice but through erosion of steady employment, outsourcing, downsizing, and strategic layoffs by their former employers.

This highly mobilized workforce model is likely to be more and more prevalent in the future. Will you need problem solving skills in this highly fluid work landscape? YES!

Consulting

The field of consulting had traditionally dealt with helping companies and other organizations with strategy and with solving problems. There are still some excellent consulting firms that do this, some of which operate internationally. In recent years, however, a large portion of consulting activities that businesses have sought have been associated with training and outsourcing. Companies have outsourced many activities that they used to hire employees to perform. These activities also include training. Through outsourcing activities that are not in the core business but are subject to change, especially rapid change, a company can place the burden and cost of keeping current with a contractor specializing in this area. Given the large talent pool in the mobile workforce and the plethora of new problems that are emerging and will continue to emerge, not to mention the degree of specialization that has occurred, it is likely that the field of consulting will move more toward problem solving in the future.

26

Where this is all leading
(or, the next singularity)

The accelerating pace of expansion of new technology will not only create greater productivity, and more problems, but it may be leading to the next singularity. The term "singularity" may be defined as an event or point in time where our old models must be discarded and a new reality is manifest. There is a belief among many artificial intelligence experts, computer scientists, and others that there is a coming "singularity" or development in technology that will dramatically transform human civilization as radically as the previous well known and well-studied singularities: the agricultural revolution and the industrial revolution.

Prior to the agricultural revolution, humans were hunters and gatherers. The agricultural revolution lasted for 10,000 years and created farms, enabling food to be generated under controlled conditions and changing the way civilizations were organized as well as forming entirely different social structures. The industrial revolution, lasting for more than 200 years up to the present time, displaced many farmers and farm workers, dramatically reduced the number of farms, and magnified our capability to manufacture, revolutionized transportation and communication, created medical devices and drugs, and unimaginably lethal weapons of war.

The "next singularity" or the "coming singularity" was forecast by Vernor Vinge in March 1993 at a symposium sponsored by NASA Lewis Research Center and the Ohio Aerospace Institute and has since been written about and debated extensively. His vision is that a transformation of civilization, the next singularity, will take place when machine intelligence (or alternatively human intelligence amplified by machines or biological processes) exceeds existing human intelligence and that the consequent transformation will be as profound and extensive as for the prior singularities. We may be seeing the early stages of this transformation right now.

Whether civilization experiences another singularity or not, there is much speculation as to how societal changes will all play out as machine intelligence evolves, and one can spend days reviewing the opinions of various experts. According to Moore's law, for example, the sheer number of computing elements (transistors) on a computer chip (of a given size) will continue to double about every two years for some time to come. Today's laptop computers are about as intelligent as a lizard's brain in terms of the number of operations per second that can be performed. As hardware capability continues to grow and software continues to evolve, it is predicted that machine intelligence will eventually surpass human intelligence.

There is a lot of debate as to what intelligence is also. Perhaps in the not too distant future, you will answer a phone call from an intelligent machine trying to sell you a product and will have difficulty in determining that your caller is not human. Asking a trivia question may not work, as Watson has demonstrated. One way to tell might be to give the caller a simple brain teaser. The ability to solve problems that are not addressable by simple logic and in fact may call upon human experience will be a daunting task for any machine capable of speech recognition and will not come about any time soon.

There is no doubt that Artificial Intelligence or "AI", or in other words "intelligent machines", is continuing to expand. Simultaneously, however, Intelligence Amplification or "IA", a term coined by Vinge and representing human intelligence enhanced by machines, is also continuing to expand. IA may also include biological enhancement of human intelligence or perhaps enhancement of intelligence by connecting the brain with a bio chip to increase memory or other capabilities. Whether AI or IA reigns supreme, at some point civilization will most likely change beyond anyone's ability to predict it. So how will these changes, if they occur, impact problem solving?

For the time being and for the foreseeable future, the unique ability of humans to recognize and to solve big, important problems falls outside of the domain of computerized systems and perhaps even artificial intelligence-based computer systems of the most advanced types. If you want to solve BIPs, you will probably need to involve other people as well as machines. Even Albert Einstein involved others. So, you should not worry. In fact, computers and people with computers will continue to enhance your problem solving activities.

Thinking alongside machines

A college professor friend of mine from Iowa recently shared a striking observation with me. He said that during a period of time around 10 years ago, he noticed that, as he put it, his students *stopped thinking.* I normally wouldn't have taken much notice to such an outlandish claim, but I had heard the same thing a few years earlier from another college professor friend of mine from North Carolina. Barry, the professor from Iowa, said that the point when his students *stopped thinking* coincided with the spreading use of computers, in particular with students starting to bring laptops into the classroom. He recalled that when he saw students using laptops to look up homework and test answers via Google, a new paradigm was established.

Barry's conjecture was that with the easy access to Google, students are now spending less time *thinking* and *problem solving* and more time simply looking up answers. If this is true, if in fact the students of today are not learning to really solve problems, then we're in trouble. Growth of the economy and innovation and the creation of new technologies, new business models, and new social and humanitarian initiatives are all the result of thinking and problem solving. If we lose this ability our country will experience economic decline. Hopefully, parents will teach their children the value of thinking and problem solving, and our schools will keep up.

Does this mean that computer, internet, and cell phone technology are hindering problem solving? Definitely not! Technology has always enhanced problem solving. It is important to embrace technology and use it in new ways. New, unprecedented opportunities are opening. We are at the beginning of an era that will require using technology in ever newer and more creative ways, an era where technology is already generating new business models, such as Facebook and Twitter, and will lead to new paradigms for innovation. The combination of Dragonfly Thinking and technology is the most powerful.

Genuine curiosity is a human trait which we don't understand very well, and have no clue how to program into a computer. But it is one of the most basic features of the way that we think, and it underlies nearly all great movements and discoveries. Computers will continue to be critical in executing the demands of our curiosity, but the day is still far off when the computers themselves will be asking questions out of their own interest. Even with many answers available to us on the web, we must be able to ask our own questions, and do our own, very deliberate thinking, if we are to create the great innovations of the future.

As a simple example, Problem Number 5 – the brain teaser – in Appendix 2 in this book was discovered by a computer scientist while solving another problem using a computer to search through a vocabulary file. It aroused his curiosity. The resulting brain teaser, Problem Number 5 that came out of this curiosity, is an extremely difficult brain teaser to solve without a very good clue or without the aid of a computer. Computers can aid the search through files and through data and manipulate data in many ways; but computers are really not part of Nature and did not evolve by fighting their way through the environment to survive. Consequently, they do not have many features that the human has and that even the dragonfly probably has, such as curiosity.

Crowdsourcing

An interesting approach to problem solving involving experts is *crowdsourcing*, a web-based problem solving and production model, in which a problem is broadcast to an unknown group of solvers in the form of an open call for solutions. DARPA (Defense Advanced Research Projects Agency), an agency of the US Department of Defense (and also the originator of the project that created the internet), has used this crowdsourcing approach in a number of projects and challenges. At the end of October 2009, DARPA moored 10, eight-foot red weather balloon markers at fixed locations across the United States and challenged teams to be first to report the location of all of the balloons. Collaboration of efforts was required to complete the challenge quickly, and the winning team (MIT, in less than seven hours!!) established its own collaborative environment to win.

Stackoverflow.com is a web site that posts questions in computer programming for anyone, professional or amateur, to address. This is another example of collaboration – giving anyone the opportunity to fill a common need and in the process to gain some respect or recognition.

Other crowdsourcing initiatives abound. InnoCentive (inno-centive.com), in Waltham, Massachusetts is a crowdsourcing organization that signs up companies and scientific problem solvers. Companies are willing to pay for solutions, and the "crowd" is charged with suggesting solutions to very specified problems. The problems circling on this internet problem-oriented marketplace are typically quite narrowly defined, and for this type of problem, the crowdsourcing solution seems to work.

Other marketplaces include: Yet2.com, also in Needham Massachusetts, a specific technical problem oriented web site seeking novel solutions as well as providing a place to post novel solutions looking for problems; IdeaConnection.com in Vancouver British Columbia, an industrial problem oriented site; NineSigma.com in Cleveland Ohio, an open innovation service provider; TopCoder.com in Glastonbury Connecticut, an open innovation software design internet community; and others.

Problem solvers, please note: Crowdsourcing approaches external to your organization are not your competitors. They are not serious sources of competition for you in your efforts to solve problems in your organization. The primary reason for this is that rarely will a company or other organization go outside to "unknown" individuals to solve its key problems. You do not have to worry that your BIP will fall prey to a crowdsourcing competitor. Typically, a BIP is something that stays within a company and is resolved internally. It's like in the saying: "What happens in Vegas stays in Vegas". Most of the time, companies have not defined their BIPs well enough to post a question on a crowdsourcing site, anyway – even if they wanted to. More likely, when a key problem is discovered that must be solved, and it has been determined that outside help is necessary, a specific consultant or a consulting group is called in, typically in the strictest of confidence.

Problem solving and people skills

A company is a domain for workers and managers. It is often preferred to solve a company's problems within the realm of the company, as this approach is usually the most cost effective and the most private. It is also common, however, for a company's employees to not actually know where some of the company's fundamental problems lie. *This is where* **you** *come in*. Recognizing and finding viable solutions to problems is a way to add considerably more value than you're being paid for, often through merely a side-effort. This can lead you to future opportunities and advancement in the organization.

As a company grows and evolves, things change. Some problems are solved, but new ones emerge. Even small changes in the way business is done inevitably generate new problems. For example, this can happen when new technology is introduced. Because of the complexity of how problems can emerge and hide away, there may be others in your company who are better positioned than you to notice new BIPs.

Therefore, *maintaining contact with people in your company who can help you to identify new problems is essential*. Developing the skills to work with others in finding and tackling problems is a key to success.

If you want to solve big important problems you will probably need to involve other people.

If you want to solve big important problems quickly, you ***must*** *involve other people!*

In the future, problem solving will continue to consist of sincere and meaningful interactions between people for common goals: defining and understanding problems, brainstorming to generate ideas and possible solutions, determining whether a proposed solution is viable or workable, and finally, implementing a chosen and validated solution. Implementing the solutions to problems is not covered here, but it also involves people and tends to be organization-specific. It requires awareness of the culture of your organization, as well as buy-in from individuals at your level, above you and below you.

Interactions with others drives problem solving. This is true whether you gather a group in a room for formal brainstorming sessions, or even if you just informally meet people for coffee. The *people* component is essential in solving big important problems, and individuals who develop problem solving capabilities and *also* interact effectively with others are the architects of change and growth, the innovators and implementers. These innovators will be highly sought after, and their contributions will be well recognized. If you achieve a problem solving track record, rest assured your services will be in demand.

27

Ongoing use of what this book teaches

Gaining domain experience in a particular business or technology is a matter of detailed study and experience in that realm. Solving difficult problems in technology development or in business, however, requires different sets of skills. If you are a good problem solver, you can often work with someone with domain experience, to solve the most difficult of problems that arise. Sometimes, however, solving these problems is achieved far more easily by consulting with a person who has solved similar problems. I have been developing technology since I was in high school. Solving complex business and technology problems came much later on. When I started a new company, I faced problems that were entirely foreign to me.

Flash Case Study: Stuck!

I have had many great mentors in technology development and business. One of my greatest business mentors was Eugene Kleiner, Founder of the venture capital (VC) firm Kleiner Perkins Caufield & Byers (considered one of the top VC firms). In 1986, after I founded a company called Cardiovascular Diagnostics,

Eugene advised my venture capital lead investors to go ahead and invest in my company, and he became a limited partner in the local VC investment fund and also became an advisor to me. I soon learned that the solutions to some problems are relatively simple if you have the right experience, as Eugene had.

We were developing a small, portable device for bedside or home use to monitor blood thinners, known medically as anticoagulant drugs – the drugs that save lives by preventing lethal blood clots from forming. These drugs must be monitored periodically, since failure to do so could result in either insufficient therapy (leading to blood clots) or excessive anticoagulation (leading to internal bleeding). I had contributed to this field while still a college student, in my first biomedical project, by developing a laboratory instrument, but developing this portable device was a different and more difficult problem. We were about six months away from finalizing our product, when I discovered at a trade show that another company was introducing a product similar to the one we were developing.

Until that moment, I thought that our product would be the first of its kind on the market, but I was wrong. Here was another company that had made a similar product using an entirely different technology. It was a different technological development, yielding a product with the same purpose. The other company already had product literature and would soon be shipping their product to customers. I wasn't sure what to do.

I spoke with my lead investors. They were quite upset but offered no solutions or advice that would be helpful. I was afraid they were going to pull the plug on my company and not continue to fund it. Then I spoke with Eugene Kleiner. He looked at the product literature from the competing company and stared at the picture of the device they were introducing. He then said very calmly: "Well, now we have one of these. We don't really need another, do we?" I was a bit afraid of what might come next and wasn't sure where he was going, but he continued: "Their product does only one type of diagnostic test, or possibly two. How about putting more tests on your device? Then you'll be offering something different."

That night I got to work, and before too long our product had five relevant medical diagnostic tests on it. In retrospect, the advice from Eugene Kleiner was so very simple. It solved a problem that I had lost sleep over and that my lead investors, who were good business people, were at a loss to solve.

There is a saying that: *'Smart business people learn from their mistakes and never make the same mistake again, but wise business people consult with smart business people and do not make the mistakes in the first place.'*

Today, the technology we developed is used all over the world. Roche Diagnostics uses it in a product called the CoaguChek[R] system that is sold to monitor Coumadin[R] and other warfarin drugs. Coumadin is perhaps the most widely used prescription cardiovascular drug in the US. The Roche CoaguChek product is a hand-held device, like a glucose meter, in use for monitoring these drugs in hospitals, physician's offices, clinics, and in the home. Other companies, such as Helena Laboratories, Inc. in the US and A & T Corporation in Japan, use the technology that we developed to perform a variety of diagnostic tests on relatively small devices. So the approach Eugene Kleiner suggested solved the problem, and enabled commercial success.

28

Go Forth and Do!

Gumption

In the cultural classic non-fiction novel "Zen and the art of Motorcycle Maintenance," Robert Persig calls the confidence to attack extremely different problems *gumption*. Nurture your *gumption*. You can start off with some easier problems to get the initial confidence, and then work your way through more difficult problems. Gumption can be seen as an energy cache that will build or deplete with experience and use.

A key point to remember, as you gather your gumption and delve into problem solving, is that you can't really learn how to solve BIPs from a book. Problem solving is like driving a car: you actually need to get behind the wheel. If you look at problem solving as an experience-driven skill, you'll realize that big results will take time, but you will eventually be successful and reap great rewards. After solving BIPs, you will be given new opportunities to solve bigger and more important problems, and ultimately to build a name and a career.

Seize the day!

CARPE DIEM

You may have heard the expression *Carpe Diem*. It means "Seize the day"!

If you are using this book properly, you will have taken action with each of the exercises, and done a little bit of the Dragonfly method on your own. This is really just a first step. But without taking the first step, you will never get to the second, or the third... Problem solving really all boils down to a series of such steps, eventually leading to solving a BIP. There is a mnemonic that you may find useful and that may help motivate you:

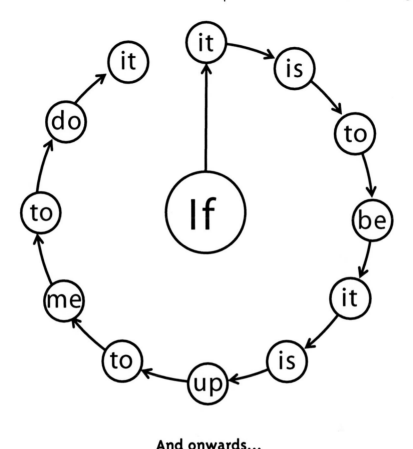

And onwards...

Good luck in your quest to identify and solve worthy problems: Big Important Problems, i.e., BIPs. I wish you the very best of luck in finding them and in solving them, and remember: the harder you work the luckier you get!

Another take home lesson from the end of Chapter 18 is that physical exercise and relaxation will help also, often when least expected. If you become a successful problem solver, people will notice, and watch what happens next. You will definitely create value, and as a result others will benefit, and so will you.

Oh, and by the way, thank you for bearing with me on my passion for dragonflies. Now, in case you were wondering: is the dragonfly intelligent? Perhaps not by human standards, but it has existed in the environment for hundreds of millions of years, outliving the dinosaurs and most other creatures. Today there are at least 5,500 known species of dragonflies. The dragonfly might not be intelligent by our standards, but it sure knows how to survive.

"It has yet to be proven that intelligence has any survival benefit"

— ARTHUR C. CLARKE, SCIENCE FICTION AUTHOR AND THE ONE WHO FIRST THOUGHT UP THE GEOSYNCHRONOUS SATELLITE AND THE SPACE ELEVATOR.

"It is not the strongest of the species that survives, nor the most intelligent, but the one most responsive to change."

— CHARLES DARWIN, ORIGINATOR OF THE THEORY OF EVOLUTION:

Finally, some selected quotes from Albert Einstein, one of the greatest problem solvers of all time and one of my personal heroes!

"Great spirits have always encountered violent opposition from mediocre minds"

"Look deeply into nature, and then you will understand everything better."

"We still do not know one thousandth of one percent of what nature has revealed to us."

"The true sign of intelligence is not knowledge but imagination."

"Logic will get you from A to B. Imagination will take you everywhere."

"Anyone who has never made a mistake has never tried anything new."

"It's not that I'm so smart; it's just that I stay with problems longer."

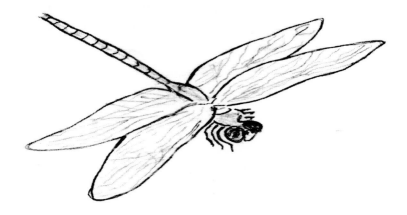

Fin.

Appendix 1:
Overview of processes, definitions and methods

Overview of Dragonfly Thinking:
Find, Study, Seek, and Solve

Stage 1: Find a BIP
> *Identify the right problem to work on.*
> *Begin to validate that it is a BIP.*

> **TACTICAL PROCESS 1:** Develop a master list of problems to be solved

> **EXERCISE 1:** Work on your list

Stage 2: **Study the BIP**
> *Validate that the problem is a BIP.*
> *Develop a passion for solving this problem*
> *Consider the problem as terrain.*
> *Fly high above the terrain to survey the problem from all angles.*
> *Swoop low on occasion and hover in a selected location to examine promising areas that could lead to a solution.*

TACTICAL PROCESS 2: Validate that solving the Big problem that you selected will be of great help to your organization

EXERCISE 2: Map your terrain

Stage 3: **Seek help from an SMC**
Generate ideas and see what others (especially an SMC) think about them.
Follow the ideas where they lead you.

TACTICAL PROCESS 3: How to cultivate the ability to develop a relationship with a sponsor, mentor, or champion (SMC)

EXERCISE 3: Make a list of potential SMCs

Stage 4: **Solve the BIP**

TACTICAL PROCESS 4: An eight-step process for problem solving:
1. *Survey the problem from different vantage points, like the dragonfly*
2. *Use domain experience & generate new ideas*
3. *Redefine the problem & generate more ideas accordingly*
4. *Recombine, link, or add to ideas*
5. *Take a break.*
6. *Consolidate ideas into groups based on similarity*
7. *Rank groups and repeat process*
8. *Select the most likely group, and work towards solution*

EXERCISE 4: Try solo problem solving with a brainteaser

General principles

A. Think deeply about a problem before starting to develop its solution.

B. Choose your problem wisely and remember: necessity is the mother of invention, but stress is often the enemy of creativity.

C. *The Iceberg Principle of Epiphanies*: By bringing a problem everywhere with you, you will vastly increase the chance of connecting the hidden dots, and finding a solution.

D. New ideas can come from anywhere.

E. Ideas are the fuel that make the impossible possible.

F. For group problem solving, start recruiting the first team member first.

Working definitions

BIP – Big Important Problem (Pronounced simply to rhyme with blip, or as BIP as in VIP)

LUP – Little Unimportant Problem (Pronounced simply to rhyme with cup or as LUP as in abc)

Decision Making – choosing the one option that will yield the most favorable outcome, given a number of possible choices.

Troubleshooting – correcting a situation in which an ongoing process or a system has an unexpected failure.

Problem Solving – finding a satisfactory solution to a dilemma, a puzzle, a perplexing situation, or an impediment to growth or to progress, given no apparently good options.

Innovation – creating something new that can be actualized, typically in the physical world. Innovation often but not necessarily results from solving a problem.

SMC – **Sponsor, Mentor, or Champion**

Sponsor – An individual who agrees to provide resources to help you.

Mentor – An individual who helps you with your career.

Champion – An individual who wants to see it happen or help make it happen.

APPENDIX 2:
Additional Brainteasers

Extra brainteasers

1. The Hotel Room – Three sailors on shore leave at a sparsely populated island decided to rent a hotel room. They went to the registration desk and asked for the price of a room. They were told: $30. Each sailor handed over $10, got the key, and went up to the room. When they arrived in the room, there was a knock on the door, and the bell hop was standing outside. He said: "There was a mistake. The room is not $30; it is only $25. I have $5 change for you." He apologized for the mistake and then asked how they were going to divide $5 between three guys. They hesitated, so the bell hop said: "How about each of you takes $1 and gives the remaining $2 to me as a tip". The sailors agreed, and the bell hop took his $2 and left. The sailors then thought: Each of us paid $9. The total of $9 x 3 is $27, plus the $2 we gave to the bell hop is $29. What happened to the 30th dollar?

2. The Great Diamond Robbery (repeated from Chapter 17) – A crafty criminal was being chased by the police. He was carrying a small sack of diamonds that he had just stolen from a diamond dealer. He ran past a street

corner where two little boys were selling lemonade. There were three large pitchers of lemonade and a stack of cups. The sign read: "Lemonade for Sale 15 Cents per Cup," and a smaller sign read: "All Proceeds will be used for our School Science Project". In a flash, the criminal dropped all of the diamonds into an opened ice chest that the boys were using. The diamonds were completely lost in the ice and could not be seen. Two policemen arrived seconds later and apprehended the criminal but could not locate the diamonds. One of the policemen asked the boys if they had seen any diamonds. Without saying a word, within 10 seconds one of the boys handed the policeman a whole bunch of diamonds, separated from the ice. How did he do this, and what was the school science project probably about?

3. The Three Wise Men – A king had three wise men as his most trusted advisors. He wanted to find out which one was the wisest of the three. He devised the following test. All three wise men were blindfolded and asked to pick a hat from a box containing three white hats and two black hats. He then removed the box with the remaining two hats from the room and asked the first wise man to remove his blindfold and to determine, by looking at the hats of the others, his own hat color. The first wise man removed his blindfold but could not guess his own hat color. The second wise man likewise did the same, but he could not guess his own hat color either. The third wise man then removed his blindfold and quickly determined his hat color. What did he see, and how did he determine his hat color? (This one may take a little while, but you should know when you achieve the right answer.)

4. The Butcher Shop – A woman goes to the butcher to buy a pound of chopped meat. She places her order and notices that the butcher places a one pound weight

on one arm of a balance-type scale and weighs out the meat on the opposing arm of the scale. She then notices that the arm of the scale where the meat is situated is longer than the arm where the one pound weight rests. Recalling her experiences with a seesaw, where her young son could balance her if he moved further out from the center and she moved closer, she knew immediately that she might not be getting a full pound of meat. She complained to the butcher. He said: "OK if you buy two pounds of meat, I will reverse the positions of the one pound weight and the meat for the second weighing." The butcher did exactly as he said he would in the second weighing and packaged the meat from the second weighing with the first and charged the woman for two pounds of meat. When the woman got home, she said: "Did I really buy two pounds of meat; or did I buy less than two pounds of meat; or did I buy more than two pounds of meat?" How much meat did she buy and why?

5. A Mysterious Word – What familiar 13 letter word has 5 copies of one letter, 4 copies of a second letter, 2 copies of a third letter, and a single copy each of two additional letters? (This one is quite difficult, and if you correctly identify the word, congratulations! You can now consider yourself a member of a very, very small but elite group.)

6. The Fishermen – If a man and a half can catch a fish and a half in a day in a half, how many fish will six men catch in seven days?

7. The House and the Furnace – There is a house and a furnace. The house is twice as old as the furnace was when the house was as old as the furnace is now. How old is the house, and how old is the furnace?

Solutions to extra brainteasers

1. The Hotel Room – Each sailor paid $10 but received $1 back. Therefore, the cash outlay was $9 each. The total cash outlay was $9 x 3 or $27. Of the $27, $25 went to the hotel for the room, and $2 went to the bell hop. There was no 30th dollar. There was not even a 29th or 28th dollar.

2. The Great Diamond Robbery – The boy scooped up several handfuls of ice from the ice chest and added them to a pitcher of lemonade. The ice floated, and the diamonds sank quickly to the bottom. The boy then reached into the pitcher, grabbed a small handful of diamonds from the bottom, and offered them to the policeman. The school science project was about buoyancy and density.

3. The Three Wise Men – The third wise man wore a white hat. The first wise man saw either two white hats or a white and a black hat; otherwise he would have seen two black hats and won the contest on the spot. The second wise man, likewise, must have seen a white and a black hat or two white hats. The third wise man knew this and realized that if he had a black hat on his head, the second wise man would have seen this and known immediately his own hat color was white – otherwise the first wise man would have seen two black hats and won. Therefore the hat color of the third wise man had to be white.

4. The Butcher Shop – The woman bought more than two pounds of meat. This is why: to achieve balance on a seesaw or balance-type scale, the downward force (amount of weight) at one end multiplied by its moment arm (distance of the weight from the pivot point or center of the balance scale) must equal the downward force at

the other end multiplied by its moment arm. If the arms are of unequal lengths, we can call these lengths L_1 and L_2, where L_1 is greater than L_2. For the first weighing, we have the following equation: $L_1 \times M_1 = L_2 \times (1)$, where: M_1 is the weight of the meat in pounds in the first weighing, and (1) is one pound (the one pound weight). Solving for M_1, we have: $M_1 = [L_2/L_1] \times (1) = L_2/L_1$. For the second weighing, we have the following equation: $L_1 \times (1) = L_2 \times M_2$, where: M_2 is the weight of the meat in pounds in the second weighing, and (1) is one pound (the one pound weight). Solving for M_2, we have: $M_2 = [L_1/L_2] \times (1) = L_1/L_2$. **Since the total meat purchased is $M_1 + M_2$, this is equal to $L_2/L_1 + L_1/L_2$. But this result is the sum of a number (L_2/L_1) plus its reciprocal (L_1/L_2). The sum of any number plus its reciprocal is always greater than 2, for example: 3/2 + 2/3 = 13/6 or 5/4 + 4/5 = 41/20, etc. The only exception is the number 1, which is exactly equal to its reciprocal, where 1/1 + 1/1 = 2, but for this to be the case and for the woman to have received exactly 2 pounds of meat, the balance arms (L_1 and L_2) would have had to have been equal, but this was not the case.**

5. A Mysterious Word – "Sleeplessness"

6. The Fishermen – Six men will catch 28 fish in seven days. [If 1.5 men catch 1.5 fish in 1.5 days, then 3 men catch 3 fish in 1.5 days. So, 6 men catch 6 fish in 1.5 days. Therefore, 6 men catch 4 fish in 1 day. Finally, 6 men can catch 4 x 7 = 28 fish in 7 days.]

7. The House and the Furnace – The furnace is ¾ the age of the house, but the exact ages cannot be determined. For example, if the house is now 4 years old, the furnace would be 3 years old. When the house was 3 years old, the furnace was 2, so the house is now twice as old as the furnace was back then. If the house is now 40 years old, the furnace would be 30 years old.

For more on

Dragonfly Thinking:

Problem Solving for a Successful Future

go to:

www.bjobiomedical.com